The Operetta Book

Also by John Drinkrow
The Musical Comedy Book

The Operetta Book

by John Drinkrow

DRAKE PUBLISHERS INC   NEW YORK

ISBN 0 87749 529 7
LCCCN 73-3707
Published in 1973 by
Drake Publishers Inc
381 Park Avenue South
New York, N.Y. 10016

Printed in Great Britain

Contents

8

Illustrations

Introduction

Anyone who picks up this book will see at a glance that all the works included, though many are familiar under English titles and in English-language versions, originated in France, Austria or Germany. This is not to suggest that operetta is the sole preserve of these countries: there have been many English, American, Russian, Spanish, Bulgarian, Rumanian, and other operettas, which would undoubtedly have found their way into a bigger volume. My limited objective has been to present brief details of the origins, plots, principal numbers and international discography of some fifty vintage works which are still performed on the professional or amateur stage, or are known to record collectors. A companion volume in preparation will deal with works which originated in England and America, embracing operetta, light opera, musical comedy and the present-day 'musical'. The Gilbert and Sullivan collaboration has already been accorded a volume of its own: Michael Hardwick's *Osprey Guide to Gilbert and Sullivan,* published in 1972.

Where, after all, lies the division between operetta and these other forms? Despite all attempts to fix it precisely, there is always a residue of works which insist upon straying across the boundaries. Rather than try to be dogmatic in an essentially devil-may-care medium, I have cheerfully made my own choice within the scope permitted by a volume of a certain size and price. I have, however, gratefully heeded two advisers: Miss Leila Mackinlay, speaking for the theatregoer, and Mr Frank Rogers, representing record collectors. Details of Mr Rogers's contribution will be found at the head of the Discography. Miss Mackinlay is the daughter of the late Sterling Mackinlay, who was so well known in the field of light opera and wrote the monumental *Origin and Development of Light Opera* (Hutchinson, 1927); she has been writing on the subject for many years in the journal *Amateur Stage* and elsewhere, and has herself adapted and presented many operettas.

I am also grateful to the following: Mr John Hughes, director of the National Operatic and Dramatic Association; Mr Roy Stacey, editor of *Amateur Stage;* the Johann Strauss Society of Great Britain, and in particular its honorary librarian, Mr Leonard A. Hawkey; Mr Tom Hammond and Mr Ronald Brooks, respectively music consultant and music librarian of the Sadler's Wells Opera Company, and their staff; the staff of the British Broadcasting Corporation's Reference Library, Gramophone Library and Music Library; and Raymond Mander and Joe Mitchenson, who made illustrations of the London productions available from their celebrated collection. I should like also to acknowledge the assistance given by Messrs. Josef Weinberger Ltd., Glocken Verlag Ltd. and Octava Music Co. Ltd., the copyright owners of a number of the operettas in this volume, by whose permission the synopses and lyric examples are included; their initials are shown against the relevant works.

Readers in search of details of many operettas not included here could not do better than go to Mark Lubbock's *The Complete Book of Light Opera* (Putnam, 1962); and an excellent and often amusing musicological study is *Composers of Operetta* by Gervase Hughes (Macmillan, 1962).

One final word should be added. Readers of this book might well find curious divergences of characters' names and certain plot details between my accounts and performances which they see. This is not the result of aberration: operettas are often presented in versions specially simplified or amended for amateur performance and for English comprehension, in some of which some characters' names are changed and others retained. My details are drawn from the professional – and generally the original Continental – versions.

Alphabetical List of Operettas

In the body of this book the operettas have been grouped under the names of their respective composers. The title shown is the original, in French or German; but where the name by which the work is well known in England is not the same – or not near enough to be obvious – I have shown the English equivalent in brackets.

The list which follows here is intended for English eyes, using the title by which I believe the work will be best recognized here. The discography at the end of the volume employs full cross-reference between original and English titles and includes some equivalents in other languages in which listed recordings are to be found.

Beautiful Galatea, The (Die Schöne Galatea) – Suppé
Beggar Student, The (Der Bettelstudent) – Millöcker
Belle Hélène, La (The Lovely Helen) – Offenbach
Bird-Seller, The (Der Vogelhändler) – Zeller
Boccaccio – Suppé
Cagliostro in Wien (Cagliostro in Vienna)
  – Johann Strauss II
Chocolate Soldier, The (Der Tapfere Soldat) – Oscar Straus
Circus Princess, The (Die Zirkusprinzessin) – Kálmán
Cloches de Corneville, Les (The Bells of Corneville)
  – Planquette

Count of Luxembourg, The (Der Graf von Luxemburg)
– Lehár

Countess Maritza, The (Die Gräfin Mariza) – Kálmán

Czarevich, The (Der Zarewitsch) – Lehár

Dollar Princess, The (Die Dollarprinzessin) – Fall

Drum-Major's Daughter, The (La Fille du Tambour-Major)
– Offenbach

Dubarry, The (Die Dubarry) – Millöcker

Fille de Madame Angot, La (Madame Angot's Daughter)
– Lecocq

Fledermaus, Die (The Bat) – Johann Strauss II

Frasquita – Lehár

Frau Luna (Castles in the Air) – Lincke

Frederica (Friederike) – Lehár

Giuditta (Judith) – Lehár

Grand Duchess of Gérolstein, The (La Grande-Duchesse
de Gérolstein) – Offenbach

Gypsy Baron, The (Der Zigeunerbaron) – Johann Strauss II

Gypsy Love (Zigeunerliebe) – Lehár

Gypsy Princess, The (Die Czardasfürstin) – Kálmán

Land of Smiles, The (Das Land des Lächelns) – Lehár

Lilac Domino, The (Der Lila Domino) – Cuvillier

Lilac Time (Das Dreimäderlhaus) – Schubert

Little Duke, The (Le Petit Duc) – Lecocq

Little Michus, The (Les P'tites Michu) – Messager

Madame Pompadour – Fall

Mam'zelle Nitouche – Hervé

Mascotte, La (The Mascot) – Audran

Merry War, The (Der Lustige Krieg) – Johann Strauss II

Merry Widow, The (Die Lustige Witwe) – Lehár

Monsieur Beaucaire – Messager

Night in Venice, A (Eine Nacht in Venedig) – Johann
Strauss II

The Operettas

Viktoria und ihr Husar *(Victoria and her Hussar) by Paul Abraham, libretto by Alfred Grünewald and Fritz Löhner-Beda, from the Hungarian of Emmerich Földes. First produced: Vienna, 1930; London, 1931. English book by Harry Graham. Set in Siberia, Japan, Russia and Hungary, soon after the First World War.*

Viktoria's Hussar is Colonel Stefan Koltay, whom she had believed killed in the war. Lonely and heartbroken, she had gratefully married John Cunlight, now American Ambassador to Japan. But at an Embassy party she is astonished to see Stefan. He and his servant Jancsi had been taken prisoners of war, escaped from Siberia, and reached Japan, where Stefan had chanced to see Viktoria and tracked her down to the Embassy, to whose party he has gained admittance under the name of Czaky, a Hungarian anxious to return to his homeland. John Cunlight has been posted to St Petersburg, and he insists on 'Czaky' accompanying him and Viktoria on the journey.

Viktoria tries to avoid Stefan's company. At length, in the Embassy at St Petersburg, he manages to ask her to come away with him, but her gratitude for her husband's kindness will not let her, and she asks him to go. Hearing that the Russians have become aware of his identity, he gives away his whereabouts to them and they arrive to arrest him. He explains to Viktoria that he cannot accept the protection of the man who holds her as his wife, and is marched away. John Cunlight recognises the depth of Viktoria's love for Stefan. At the start of their marriage he had promised that if anything should come between them he would set her free without bitterness. Now he does so.

For a year, Viktoria wanders the world, trying to enjoy

herself and wondering whether she will ever hear of Stefan again. Eventually she returns to her home village in Hungary. It is Harvest Festival, a time when marriage vows are made or renewed. Viktoria's brother Feri and O Lia San, the Japanese-French bride he had found while visiting the Tokyo Embassy, are one couple who renew their vows; and Stefan's servant Jancsi and Viktoria's maid Riquette are among the newly betrothed. Sad amongst so much happiness, Viktoria suddenly sees John Cunlight approaching. She prepares to tell him that she will return to him, but at that moment Stefan also appears. The unselfish Cunlight has worked tirelessly to secure the release of the man whom his wife loves, and now watches wistfully as they run together to embrace.

PRINCIPAL NUMBERS

Act 1   'Pardon, madam' (Viktoria and Cunlight)
   'A modest maid' (O Lia San and Chorus)
   'Mama' (O Lia San and Feri)
   'Land of song' (Jancsi and Riquette)
Act 2   'Do – Do' (Feri and Riquette)
   'Star of my night' (Viktoria and Stefan)
   'Mousie' (O Lia San and Feri)
   'Good-night' (Viktoria and Stefan)
   'Follow the drum' (Jancsi and Riquette)
Act 3   'No time for anyone but you' (Jancsi and Riquette)

La Mascotte *(The Mascot) by Edmond Audran, libretto by Alfred Duru and Henri Chivot. First produced: Paris, 1880; London, 1881. English version by H. B. Farnie and Robert Reece. Set in 17th-century Italy.*

The mascot is a goose-girl, Bettina, whose arrival at Rocco's farm in the state of Piombino results in an impressive reversal of Rocco's characteristic bad luck. Unwisely, he mentions her beneficent influence to the old Prince Laurent, who comes hunting on his land. Things have been going badly for Laurent too, and he persuades Bettina to come back to his Court and live as a lady. Although sad to have to leave behind Pippo, her shepherd sweetheart, she cannot resist the chance.

Bettina proves a great success at Court, and Prince Laurent's fortunes undergo the hoped-for improvement. He has learnt that the powers of such mascots only last while they remain virgins, and he proposes to marry her in order to keep her intact. Pippo, however, is determined to get her back, and arrives as one of a troupe of dancers. Bettina is willing to escape with him, and they change into country clothes in readiness; but Pippo is recognised by a Pisan, Prince Fritellini, who makes him believe that Bettina is already Prince Laurent's mistress. Pippo is only too ready to cease pursuing her, and willingly responds to the advances of Laurent's daughter, Princess Fiametta, who is Fritellini's fiancée.

A double wedding ceremony is quickly arranged for Laurent and Bettina, Pippo and Fiametta. The two couples approach an altar set up in the Grand Salon, when Bettina and Pippo catch one another's glance and know that they are still in love. Before anyone can stop them they have hurled themselves through the open windows and are swimming the river boundary to the Principality of Pisa, from where, by the rules of sanctuary, they cannot be fetched back.

Pisa and Piombino go to war. Prince Fritellini leads the Pisan army and enjoys victory all the way, largely because his troops include the mascot Bettina, dressed as a boy, and Pippo, whose valour has earned him Major's rank. Without Bettina's lucky influence, Laurent has no chance and he and Fiametta have assumed the roles of wandering musicians. Fritellini learns of this, forgives Fiametta for jilting him and offers her marriage. Again, a double wedding is arranged, this time for Fritellini and Fiametta, Pippo and Bettina. Prince Laurent is an unhappy onlooker, but Pippo assures him that a mascot's powers are hereditary, and it will not be too long before a successor to Bettina arrives on the scene to bring them all good luck.

PRINCIPAL NUMBERS

Act 1   'The Mascot' (Pippo and Chorus)
        'Hands off' (Bettina)
        'Give me the Swain' (Fiametta)
        'Glou, glou' – 'The turkey's song is sweet' (Bettina and Pippo)
Act 2   'Oh, she is charming' (Pages and Chorus)
        'Oh, give me back' (Bettina)
        'Let the Nautch-girls' – Saltarello (Pippo)
        'Love is blind' (Fritellini)
Act 3   'Tis the tap of the drum' (Fritellini)
        'Mine own' (Pippo)

Im Weissen Rössl *(White Horse Inn) by Ralph Benatzky, lyrics by Robert Gilbert, book by Hans Mueller and Erik Charell, from a farce by Blumenthal and Kadelburg, and with additional numbers by Robert Stolz, Robert Gilbert, Bruno Granichstaedten, and Hans von Frankowski. First performed: Berlin, 1930; London, 1931. English version by Harry Graham. Set in the Salzkammergut region of Austria, before the First World War.*

The tourist season is at its height at the White Horse Inn, but, despite the bustle, the landlady, Josefa Vogelhuber, is looking forward to the arrival of one particular guest, Dr Erich Siedler, a lawyer. He comes every year, and Josefa, who wants him to ask her to marry him and take her away to city life, has reserved him her best room. Dr Siedler has a rival in Leopold Branmeyer, head waiter at the hotel, who discovers that the lawyer is acting for one Sülzheimer in a lawsuit against another of the hotel's guests, a peppery manufacturer named Wilhelm Giesecke, who has his daughter Ottilie with him. Hoping to divert Siedler's interests from Josefa, Leopold hints to Ottilie that the lawyer is interested in her and that by responding she could influence him to make his client press less hard upon her father.

Josefa hears something of this and sacks Leopold. Soon after, Dr Siedler approaches Giesecke with a proposal from his client that his son, Sigismund Sülzheimer, be married to Ottilie Giesecke, as a move towards settling their dispute. Giesecke agrees to interview Sigismund; but when the boy arrives he shows no interest in Ottilie, though the lisping daughter of another guest, Professor Hinzelmann, attracts him hugely. This suits Siedler well enough, for Leopold had not been exaggerating the lawyer's interest in Ottilie.

Leopold himself enjoys a happier turn of fortune by discovering that the Emperor Franz Josef is proposing to stay at the White Horse Inn. Josefa begs Leopold to resume his job for this important occasion. He is even invited to speak the address of welcome to His Majesty, but breaks down in the middle of it when he sees Josefa and Siedler, who happen to be standing together. The Emperor finds out the reason for Leopold's distress and takes it upon himself to assure Josefa that she is wasting her emotions upon Dr Siedler, who is not the right man for her. Her place is not in the city, but at the White Horse Inn. She knows the Emperor is right; and when Leopold comes to take his leave at last, she has the sense to tell him that there is another vacancy at the inn – for a husband.

PRINCIPAL NUMBERS

Act 1   'It would be wonderful' (Leopold, Josefa and Girls)
       'The White Horse Inn' (Siedler, Josefa and Chorus)
       'Your eyes' (Siedler, Ottilie and Chorus)
Act 2   'Goodbye' (Leopold and Men) ˙
       'You too' (Siedler and Ottilie)
       'Sigismund' (Sigismund and Chorus)
Act 3   'My song of love' (Ottilie, Siedler and Chorus)

Der Lila Domino *(The Lilac Domino) by Charles Cuvillier, libretto by Emmerich von Gatti and Bela Jenbach. First produced: Vienna, 1912; London, 1918. English version by H. B. Smith. Set at Palm Beach, Florida, in contemporary times.*

Leonie Forde, a pretty but shrewd girl, has agreed to marry an elderly American millionaire, Cornelius Cleveden, though she fancies his nephew, Elliston Deyn, whom Cleveden has arranged shall marry his daughter Georgine. Aware that the millionaire has a roving eye, and determined to get his money one way or another, Leonie has persuaded him to write her a cheque for a million dollars, which he has promised to sign if during the next two days she catches him making up to another woman.

All are present at a domino ball at the Baccarat Hotel, as are three hard-up gamblers, an Englishman, the Hon. André D'Aubigny, and two friends. Carabana, the Spanish gypsy orchestra leader, who also specialises in fixing marriages for a fee, promises to find an attractive heiress available for marriage. They draw lots for the one who is to have her and share her dowry with the others, and André is chosen. Waiting for Carabana to make the introduction, he finds an enchanting girl dressed in a lilac domino asleep on a couch. He kisses her awake. Despite her indignation, she is obviously attracted by the young man stooping over her.

At a tea dance at Cleveden's house next day, André meets Georgine. He knows almost at once that it was she who was the Lilac Domino, and her denials are no more than playful. Their mutual attraction is clear as daylight, though, when Georgine learns of Carabana's bargain with the three gamblers, and of herself as the heiress he had had in mind, she believes André is merely claiming his winnings.

Everything, however, is resolved at carnival time. Georgine is reconciled to André, and Leonie succeeds in catching Cleveden in compromising utterance to another woman, gets her million-dollar cheque, and is free to marry Elliston Deyn.

Act 1 'True love will find a way' (Leonie and Elliston)
'Let the music play' (André and Guests)
'Where love is waiting' (Georgine and Baroness)
'The Lilac Domino' (Georgine, Elliston, Cleveden and Guests)

Act 2 Song of the chimes (Georgine and André)
'Ladies' day' (Ensemble)
'What is done you never can undo' (Georgine and André)

Act 3 Tarantella
'King Carnival' (Chorus)

(N.B. An additional number, often successfully interpolated in Act 3 in English versions, is 'All line up in a queue', composed by Howard Carr with lyrics by D. S. Parsons.)

Die Dollarprinzessin *(The Dollar Princess) by Leo Fall, libretto by A. M. Willner and Fritz Grünbaum, from a play by Gatti-Trotha. First produced: Vienna, 1907; London, 1909. New English version by Philip Park (1967). Set in New York and Canada in contemporary period. (J.W.)*

Alice Couder is the Dollar Princess, by virtue of being the daughter of an American millionaire, John Couder, whose office she administers. She thinks she knows what riches mean, declaring that anything – even love – can be bought when needed. Her widowed father shares her belief to some extent, and has sent his brothers to Europe to find an attractive and aristocratic lady to act as hostess at his social functions. They produce a Countess Przibiczevska, of proud Russian background, with whom Couder promptly falls in love. Unbeknown to him, she has been recognised by two of

28

his employees of European extraction – Freddy Wehrburg and Hans von Schlick – as a Berlin night club singer, Olga Libinski, who had, in fact, been Freddy's mistress. Sportingly, they do not give her away.

Freddy is in love with Alice Couder, but will not submit to the domination she feels her wealth entitles her to exercise. Hans is in love with her cousin, Daisy Gray; but John Couder disapproves of the match, and they are forced to elope. Perhaps stimulated by their example, Couder announces that very evening that he will marry his 'Countess', and invites his daughter to choose her man. To the astonishment of both, when she names Freddy she is rebuffed, on the grounds that he is not to be bought.

Freddy leaves Couder's employ and goes to Canada, where he manages to buy and resuscitate a business concern which includes some oil-wells. Within a year he has become so successful that he is able to offer to sell out to Couder. He has never stopped regretting losing Alice, and this is his chance to return to her on equal terms. Though the materialist in her tries briefly to resist, love can – and does – conquer even a Dollar Princess.

PRINCIPAL NUMBERS

Act 1   'A self-made maiden' (Alice and Chorus)
       'The riding lesson' (Daisy and Hans)
       'My dream of love' (Freddy)
       'Inspection' (Alice and Freddy)
Act 2   'Typewriting' (Alice and Freddy)
       'Follow me round' (Daisy)
       'Parisienne' (Olga and Couder)
       'The Dollar Princess' (Alice, Daisy, Hans and Freddy)
Act 3   'Reminiscence' (Daisy and Hans)

Madame Pompadour *by Leo Fall, libretto by Rudolph Schanzer and Ernst Welisch. First produced in Vienna, 1922; London, 1923. English lyrics by Harry Graham. Set in mid-18th-century Paris.*

The Marquise de Pompadour – known throughout France as Madame Pompadour, mistress of the King, Louis XV – is enjoying hearing herself insulted. A fugitive from a Court Ball, she has come with her maid Belotte, both wearing masks, to a tavern packed with carnival crowds who are listening with relish to bitingly satirical songs, sung by their composer, Joseph Calicot, about herself and the King. Enough becomes enough, however. Pompadour knows she has been followed to the place by Maurèpas, the chief of police, and she confronts him with the demand that the perpetrator of such revolutionary sentiments, and those who encourage him, be arrested. The chief does his duty, but his net includes a young man to whom the Pompadour has become attracted during the evening – René d'Estrades, a nobleman enjoying Parisian gaiety in contrast to his wife and their country life. To save him, Pompadour has to save Calicot also. She makes him Court Poet, and appoints René to her personal bodyguard.

Calicot soon finds court life and enforced patriotism galling, but is compensated by the affections of Belotte. René, meanwhile, has fallen deeply in love with the Pompadour, who now receives René's wife, Madeleine, who has come to Paris in search of him. Though Pompadour does not know at once of the relationship between Madeleine and René, she quickly recognises the relationship between Madeleine and herself: they are half-sisters. When the truth at last emerges, Pompadour has no heart to steal her sister's husband. She promises to bring them together again, which she achieves, after confusion caused by Maurèpas believing Calicot to be her illicit lover and trying to contrive that the King should catch them in the act. Madeleine and René are reunited, Calicot is granted a life pension by the King, and Pompadour casts her ambitious gaze on a handsome young officer of the King's suite.

PRINCIPAL NUMBERS

Act 1 'Some lucky man tonight' (Pompadour)
'Carnival time' (René)
'I am your subject' (René and Pompadour)
Act 2 'Joseph, oh, Joseph!' (Pompadour and Calicot)
'Love's sentry' (Pompadour and René)
'Reminiscence' (Pompadour and René)

Mam'zelle Nitouche *by 'Hervé' (Florimond Ronger), libretto by Henri Meilhac and Albert Millaud. First produced: Paris, 1883. Set in and near Paris.*

All is not what it seems at the convent school of Les Hirondelles. One of the seemingly most pious pupils, Denise de Flavigny, is only awaiting her chance to break out into the gay world; while the dedicated organist, Célestin, has a mistress named Corinne, about to play the leading role in an operetta, *Babet et Cadet,* composed by Célestin under the pseudonym Floridor.

When news arrives via the Mother Superior's brother, Major Chateau-Gibus, that Denise's parents are going to marry her to his brother officer, the Vicomte de Champlatreux, the girl is more delighted at the thought that she will be able to attend the first night of *Babet et Cadet*, the score of which she has found and virtually memorised. This she succeeds in doing, under the incognito 'Mam'zelle Nitouche', and during the first interval chances to make the acquaintance of her betrothed, without either of them realising it. She also chats with the composer, and they are seen by Corinne, who, jealous of her lover's attentions to this charming young girl, storms from the theatre, leaving the show without its leading lady. Denise is able to step forward and take over triumphantly. The Vicomte is enchanted and declares his love, but it is Célestin with whom she nearly has to spend the night; for Major Chateau-Gibus is also Corinne's lover, and has recognised Célestin as his rival. Célestin and Denise take refuge in a dressing-room from the Major's fury; they escape by the window, are arrested by a military patrol who suspect they are up to no good – and find themselves marched to the barracks and into the presence of the Vicomte de Champlatreux. Wine is brought in and merriment prevails, until the Major rushes in and Denise and Célestin again have to take to their heels.

Safely back at the convent next day, Denise resumes her pious pose. The Vicomte de Champlatreux calls, to make the embarrassed admission that, now that he has met Mam'zelle Nitouche, he has no heart for the arranged marriage with Denise. When the Mother Superior tells her this, Denise modestly asks her to let her meet the Vicomte alone. Returning to find the couple kissing fervently, the Mother Superior is first astonished, and then delighted at the devotion of a girl who can declare that she is willing to sacrifice herself in marriage to a man for the good of his soul.

Act 1 'Célestin and Floridor' (Célestin)
'The lead soldier' (Denise)
'Alleluia' (Ensemble)
'Goodbye, my dear' (Mother Superior and Pupils)
Act 2 'A sensible marriage' (Denise)
'Babet and Cadet' (Ensemble)
Act 3 'You're right, Floridor'
Fanfare song
'Story of the big box'

Die Czardasfürstin *(The Gypsy Princess) by Emmerich Kálmán, libretto by Leo Stein and Bela Jenbach. First produced: Vienna, 1915; London, 1921. New English version by Philip Park and Conrad Carter (1956). Set in Budapest and Vienna in contemporary times. (J.W.)*

Sylva Varescu, a leading Budapest entertainer known as 'The Gypsy Princess', is about to leave for an engagement in New York, together with her friend and discoverer, Count Boni Kancsianu, and friends are giving her a farewell party. A late arrival is her admirer, Prince Edwin Lippert-Weylersheim, whose father, Prince Leopold, disapproves of his consorting with an actress and has ordered him to rejoin his regiment immediately. Although he has been betrothed since childhood to his cousin, the Countess Stasi, Edwin insists before leaving on contracting to marry Sylva within two months. Sylva cancels her trip to America, and Edwin hurries away. Only now does Boni, who had been out of the room, learn what has happened, and tell Sylva of Edwin's betrothal. Bitterly disappointed, she tells him they will leave for America after all.

Two months later a party is taking place at the old Prince's palace in Vienna. Edwin and the Countess Stasi appear affectionate enough, and it seems that their engagement may be officially announced at any moment. But he is awaiting two further guests, who now arrive. They are Sylva and Boni, just back from America. In order to gain admittance, she is posing as his wife, a deception which is almost wrecked when Boni falls for Stasi at first sight and, forgetting that he is supposed to be married, proposes to her. He has to confide partially in her, whispering that the full truth of what is happening cannot be revealed for the moment.

Edwin, who knows that Sylva and Boni are not married, is able to present her to his father as his friend's wife, and the old Prince is charmed. However, Sylva takes offence, believing that Edwin is ashamed to present her in her own right. She shows the old man the marriage contract, tears it up, and leaves the palace, followed by Boni.

Edwin hurries after them to their hotel, closely followed by his father. The Prince Leopold fulminates against Boni for making advances to his son's betrothed. Boni silences him by telephoning Stasi and asking her to marry him: with the Prince listening in, she agrees enthusiastically. The Prince gives them his blessing, but will not countenance Edwin's desired union with Sylva until informed by a timely arrival, the old Count von Kerekes, that Prince Leopold's own second wife had once been an actress in the same company as Sylva. The old Prince is silenced, and Edwin and Sylva, Boni and Stasi are married in a double ceremony.

34

Act 1 'The gypsy bride' (Sylva and Chorus)
'Love is love' (Sylva and Edwin)
'Long live love' (Sylva, Edwin, Boni and Count von Kerekes)
Act 2 'The swallows' (Stasi and Men)
'A strong silent man' (Boni and Girls)
'Dream once again' (Sylva and Edwin)
'It's naughty Cupid' (Stasi and Boni)
'Love's sweet song' (Edwin and Sylva)
Act 3 'On, music, on' (Sylva, Feri and Boni)

Die Gräfin Mariza *(The Countess Maritza) by Emmerich Kálmán, libretto by Julius Brammer and Alfred Grünwald. First produced: Vienna, 1924; London, 1938. English versions by Robert Layer-Parker and Eddie Garr (1938); Janne Furch (1972). Set in Hungary in contemporary period. (O.C.)*

The beautiful, rich and forceful Countess Mariza pays one of her rare visits to her country estate and gives a party to announce her engagement to a Baron Koloman Zsupan. This is, actually, a fiction: she merely wishes to discourage her many other suitors. To her dismay, a man of that name turns up, and, to save face, Mariza has to acknowledge him as her fiancé and let her 'engagement' party continue.

One who is not invited to sit at table with the other guests is Mariza's bailiff, Bela Török, whose real identity is Count Tassilo Endrödy-Wittemburg, a Viennese who has taken the job, through lack of funds, in order to raise a dowry for his sister Lisa. Having drunk liberally with the gypsies outside, he leads them in a spirited song ('Play,

Gypsy'). The Countess, overhearing, calls for a repeat; he refuses, and is dismissed. Baron Zsupan and the other guests leave for a visit to a night club, but the Countess stays behind. She sees Tassilo preparing to leave and is attracted enough to withdraw his dismissal, thus unwittingly fulfilling a gypsy girl's prophecy that she would fall in love with a handsome young man of high birth.

Tassilo does his best to persuade the Countess Mariza to take an interest in the business affairs of her estate. She prefers to play at flirting, which leads to a genuine declaration by Tassilo. She responds, but soon afterwards finds a letter written by Tassilo to a friend, declaring his intention of raising money in terms which Mariza interprets to mean that he plans to marry her for hers. This belief is strengthened by a report that Tassilo has been seen talking affectionately with Lisa, whom, of course, Mariza does not know to be his sister. She accuses him publicly, throws money contemptuously at his feet, and sacks him again.

Despite his pride, Tassilo picks up the money for Lisa's sake and they get ready to go. It is only now that Mariza discovers the relationship between them, but her pride will not let her recant. She writes him a reference and sadly bids him good-bye. Before he and Lisa leave, Tassilo's wealthy aunt, Princess Bozena Guddenstein zu Chlumetz, arrives. Having heard of his money troubles, she has come to help him and provide him with a rich bride. Mariza's last resource is to ask Tassilo to read the reference she has given him. He does; it proves to be an offer to marry him. What could not be spoken between them has been written; and, on this occasion, the pen proves mightier than the word.

Act 1   'Vienna, my Vienna' (Tassilo)
'Gypsy music, my temptation' (Mariza and Chorus)
'Let's go to Varasdin' (Mariza and Prince Populescu)
'Come gypsy, play gypsy' (Tassilo)

Act 2   'All at once I'm drifting, floating' (Mariza and Tassilo)
'When I'm dreaming' (Lisa and Prince Populescu)
'Be mine, sweet love, be mine' (Mariza and Tassilo)

Act 3   'Proud and temperamental lady' (Lisa, Tassilo and Prince Populescu)

Die Zirkusprinzessin *(The Circus Princess) by Emmerich Kálmán, libretto by Julius Brammer and Alfred Grünwald. First produced: Vienna, 1926. Set in St Petersburg and Vienna in contemporary times. (O.C.)*

The star performer of the Stanaslavsky Circus in St Petersburg is the masked 'Mister X', whose speciality is to play a violin solo on a high wire and then leap down on to the back of a cantering horse below. Among those who have come to see him this evening are Princess Fedora Palinska, a beautiful widow, who has been instructed by the Czar to find another husband soon, and a Russian, into the bargain, so that her great wealth will remain in the country, and Prince Sergius Vladimir, who fits this specification but has been refused by Fedora. Fedora meets Mister X in the bar and they are mutually attracted, though he will not unmask or reveal his identity.

Prince Sergius, who also meets Mister X after his performance, is more successful in this respect. He learns that the man is Baron Korosow, who enjoys being a circus artiste at night. Sergius spots the affinity between Fedora

37

and Mister X, and plans to nurture it to the point where she will accept the Baron Korosow in marriage, not knowing him to be Mister X, when Sergius will be able to show her up in public in revenge for her refusal of himself.

He effects the meeting with Baron Korosow, and produces a forged letter from the Czar, ordering Fedora to marry at once. When Sergius suggests that she take the Baron as husband she is only too willing. The Baron is hesitant, but agrees, and they are married in Sergius's palace. The moment the ceremony is over Sergius triumphantly summons in the rest of the circus troupe and tells Fedora in front of everyone that the man she has married is Mister X, and that she is now a 'Circus Princess'. She is turning away from her husband in disgust at the trick he has lent himself to, when he discloses that he has yet another identity – Fedja Palinska, who, as a young Hussar officer, had loved her, only to see her marry his rich uncle instead. It is now he who walks away from her.

Their reconciliation is brought about two months later in Vienna, in an hotel owned by the mother of Toni Schlumberger, whose romance with another member of the circus, Mabel George, is the sub-plot. Fedora is dining at one table with Prince Sergius, Mister X at another. Mister X enlists the old waiter, Pelikan, to create a draught with an electric fan, causing the irritable Sergius to leave the room to fetch a scarf. Mister X at once joins Fedora, and it is plain that Sergius will find his return a waste of time.

Act 1 'Bravo, bravo, Mr Director!' (Sergius and Circus
        Director)
        'Two fairy-tale eyes' (Mister X)
        'What has happened in the world?' (Fedora)
        'Where is the sky so blue as Vienna's?' (Toni and
        Mabel)
        'Luck is all around' (Mister X and Fedora)
        'The little maids' (Toni)
        'Who will weep then?' (Mabel and Mister X)
        'Juppla, little Josephine, Juppla!' (Mister X and
        Fedora)
Act 2 'My darling, my darling' (Fedora and Mister X)
        'Come to the meadows' (Mabel and Toni)
        'Shut your window tonight!' (Mister X and Sergius)
        'Me and you, you and me!' (Mister X and Fedora)

Der Vetter aus Dingsda *(The Cousin from Nowhere)
by Eduard Künneke, libretto by Hermann Haller and Rideamus.
First produced: Berlin, 1921; London, 1923. English version
by Fred Thompson. Contemporary setting.*

For seven years, Julia de Weert, an orphan heiress, has
cherished her love for her cousin Roderick, who is in
Batavia, seeking his fortune. This does not suit her guardians, Kuhbrot and Wildenhagen, each of whom had wished
to marry her off to his heir, Augustus and Egon, respectively.
They are too late: Julia has come of age, and is free to
choose for herself. On hearing the news at her country
house, she decides to celebrate with her girl companion,
Hannchen, by giving an evening's entertainment to a tired

39

young traveller who happens to have come their way. They pretend the house is an inn, ply him with a cigar and drinks, and give him a luxurious bed for the night. He refuses to tell them his name, merely replying to their questions, 'I'm only a strolling vagabond.'

Restored by his night's hospitality, the 'tramp' elicits from Hannchen the story of Julia's love for her cousin and promptly announces that he himself is the long-absent Roderick. Julia is overjoyed to find that after seven years he is all she could have hoped to find him; but her bliss is spoiled when Egon von Wildenhagen brings a telegram from Roderick to say that he has only just sailed from Batavia. Still refusing to give his name, the impostor goes on his way.

Old Kuhbrot is alarmed to receive news that his nephew Augustus has arrived in the neighbourhood two days ago, on his way to visit him. He has not turned up yet. Now another stranger arrives at Julia's house. Hannchen receives him and they fall in love at first sight, but he tells her that he is the real Roderick. Their problem is how to make Julia release him for Hannchen. He tells Julia he is Augustus Kuhbrot, and when she makes it clear that she cares nothing for him, he reveals that he is Roderick, thus showing her that she had not been in love with the real Roderick, but only with her romantic idea of him. In fact, she realises, the unknown vagabond turns out to be much nearer her ideal than Roderick. Luckily for her, he is still around, for he is the missing Augustus Kuhbrot, and he and Julia are reunited, with the blessing of old Kuhbrot, Roderick and Hannchen.

PRINCIPAL NUMBERS

Act 1 'Magical Moon' (Julia)
     'Oh be careful!' (Julia, Hannchen and Egon)

Act 2   'Love and you' (Julia and Stranger)
        'The old and the new' (Hannchen and Egon)
        'Batavia' (Ensemble)
        'I'm only a strolling vagabond' (Stranger)
Act 3   'When the clouds roll by' (Ensemble)
        'Any high or low road' (Hannchen and 2nd
            Stranger)
        'Jack and Jill' (Hannchen and 2nd Stranger)

La Fille de Madame Angot *(Madame Angot's Daughter)*
by Charles Lecocq, libretto by Clairville, Giraudin and Konig.
First produced: Brussels, 1872; London, 1873. English version
by H. J. Byron. Set in Paris after the 1793 Revolution.

Madame Angot's name is legendary in Paris. Although
only a fishwife, she had crossed the seas in a balloon, narrowly
escaped from cannibals, and made no effort whatever to
escape the Grand Turk, in whose harem she had borne a
daughter, Clairette. This little orphan had been brought
back to Paris, adopted and well educated by some trades-
people of the Market. Now a young woman, she is in
business as a florist. The market people want her to marry
her neighbour, Pomponnet, a barber, and she has con-
sented, but her heart belongs to Ange Pitou, a poor poet
and writer of political satires, designed to rouse the people
against their government, the Directoire. In the nick of
time, Ange comes into a small fortune. The famous actress
Mademoiselle Lange, mistress of Barras, the head of the
government, has paid him to stop lampooning her in public, and now he can afford to marry Clairette. Her foster-
parents, however, insist on her marriage to Pomponnet

going through, and the only way she can find to delay it is by singing Ange's latest satire on Mademoiselle Lange and getting herself arrested.

Mademoiselle Lange is curious to meet the offender and has her brought to her house. The two women recognise one another as old schoolfriends, and Clairette confesses why she sang the song. She does not add that she wants to marry Ange Pitou, and when he in turn is brought to Mademoiselle Lange's house to explain why he had failed to keep his part of the bargain by allowing another satire to be made public, the actress is immediately attracted by him. This involves her in trouble from her secret lover, Larivaudiere, but she convinces him, without realising the truth of her words, that Ange is in love with Clairette Angot only.

Mademoiselle Lange and her two lovers, Barras and Larivaudiere, are actually conspirators against the Republican government, and she persuades them to enlist the rebel Ange in their cause. Disaster nearly strikes one night when the conspirators are in session and government Hussars burst in to arrest them. The resourceful actress pretends that, so far from plotting, she and her associates are preparing to enjoy a ball, and the Hussars are only too willing to forget duty in the interests of enjoying a gay waltz.

Clairette has discovered that Ange and Mademoiselle Lange are mutually attracted, and decides to force them apart; she writes to each, as if from the other, arranging a rendezvous, to which she also summons Larivaudiere and the Market people. As she had hoped, the actress and the writer are caught locked in each other's arms, and the two young women quarrel fiercely. But Clairette no longer wants her Ange back. Having found him capable of unfaithfulness, she is only too happy to hand him over to her rival and bring her neighbour, Pomponnet the barber, his long-awaited joy.

PRINCIPAL NUMBERS

Le Petit Duc *(The Little Duke) by Charles Lecocq, libretto by Henri Meilhac and Ludovic Halévy. First produced: Paris 1878; London, 1878. English version by S. and B. Rowe. Set in the early 18th century.*

The little Duke is fifteen years old, as is the little Duchess; and they have just undergone a marriage of convenience. The wedding dance is over; the guests have flocked into an adjoining room to gamble. The young couple sing a tender duet, from which it is obvious that they are really in love. Ladies-in-waiting arrive to take the Duchess away and, presumably, prepare her for the nuptial bed; but when the little Duke goes to join her he finds that she has been carried off to an Academy for Young Ladies where she is to remain for two years, by order of their respective guardians who

43

consider them too young for anything beyond the ceremonial stage of their marriage. The Duke blames his extraordinarily ugly tutor, Frimousse, for this setback, but has the satisfaction of hearing Montlandry, a messenger from the King, order Frimousse to proceed to the Young Ladies' Academy and take up the post of Professor of Etymology, for which he has been specially selected because he is so repulsive in appearance that no young lady will be tempted to fall in love with him. Montlandry also brings orders promoting the little Duke to Colonel of the Parthenay Dragoons. The Duke at once orders his troops to march for an undisclosed destination.

The Dragoons' objective is, of course, the Academy for Young Ladies and the Duke's purpose is to rescue his bride. The formidable Headmistress proves a match for any troop of soldiers, but the little Duke dons a country girl's dress over his uniform, pretends to be fleeing from the Dragoons' unwelcome attentions, and is admitted to the Academy. Keeping up his pretence, he charms the new professor, Frimousse, into handing over all the keys, and lets his troops in. The Duchess is found, and Frimousse is conscripted into the regiment.

Two years later the Duke and his Dragoons are at war. They arrive at a beleaguered headquarters just in time to save it. The Duke is acclaimed a hero, but this does not exempt him from the General's rule that no women shall be allowed in the camp. When his Duchess sneaks into his tent and they are overheard laughing together he is called to account and ordered to surrender his sword. But it is an empty threat; his heroism in battle has more than sufficed to outweigh the disciplinary offence. His sword is returned and, with the little Duchess at his side, he sets off on the distinguished errand of carrying news of the victory to the Court at Versailles.

44

Act 1 'I love you, my dear soul' (Duke and Duchess)
'When the trumpet sounds' (Duke)
Act 2 Singing lesson: 'Sol ré sol la ré' (Chorus)
'To arms!' (Soldiers)
Act 3 'No women' (Duke)

Die Lustige Witwe *(The Merry Widow) by Franz Lehár, libretto by Viktor Léon and Leo Stein, based on the play* L'Attaché *by Henri Meilhac. First produced: Vienna, 1905; London, 1907. English versions by Christopher Hassall (1958, Sadler's Wells) and Philip Park (1958). Set in contemporary Paris. (G.V.)*

Baron Zeta, Ambassador in Paris of the state of Pontevidrinia, is worried. His country is in financial straits, and its wealthiest subject, Hanna Glawari, known as 'The Merry Widow', is so rich and beautiful that she might well be snapped up by some foreigner and take her money abroad. Zeta wants it to stay in his country and is desperately hoping to find a Pontevidrinian male attractive and vital enough to suit the pleasure-loving Hanna as a husband. His choice is Count Danilo Danilowitsch, an attaché in the Embassy, who, however, spends most of his spare time with the *grisettes* at Maxim's restaurant and has to be virtually dragged away to attend the reception the Ambassador is giving for Hanna.

Danilo and Hanna are not strangers. He had once hoped to make her his wife, but she had married the rich old banker Glawari instead. Now, although he finds her as alluring as ever, Danilo, unwilling to be classed with the crowd of suitors who are after her fortune, declares that he will make do with Lolo, Dodo, Margot, Frou Frou and the rest of the girls at

Maxim's. He promises Zeta, however, that he will help to keep undesirable suitors at bay. For her part, Hanna finds Danilo as desirable as ever, and is determined that he shall marry her.

Baron Zeta's wife Valencienne is on the brink of an *affaire* with a French officer, Camille de Rosillon, who has written 'I love you' on her fan, which she has lost. At a further party – this time at the home of the Merry Widow, who opens the proceedings with her famous song 'Vilia, O Vilia, the witch of the wood' – Hanna comes into possession of the fan, and believes the message on it to be from Danilo to her. He remains elusive; but she catches the look of jealousy on his face when, in order to save Valencienne from being found by her husband with Camille in a summerhouse, she pretends that she herself was the lady involved, and she knows that Danilo is deeply in love with her.

Hanna has decorated her salon to resemble Maxim's and has invited the *grisettes* to give her guests a surprise entertainment, in the course of which she admits to Danilo that she had no assignation with Camille. His relief is apparent, but he still will not propose to her. She adds that, under her late husband's will, she loses all her inheritance if she marries again. Danilo proposes immediately, and is just as quickly accepted. But Hanna is doubly triumphant. The one detail she had not disclosed is that the money she loses is to go to her second husband. For all his principles, Danilo can only accept his delicious fate.

PRINCIPAL NUMBERS

Act 1   'A highly respectable wife' (Valencienne and Camille)

'I'm still a Pontevedrian' (Hanna and Chorus)

'I'm off to Chez Maxime' (Danilo)

'All's one to all men where there's gold (Hanna and Danilo)

'Come away to the ball' (Hanna and Danilo)

Act 2   'Vilia' (Hanna)

'Jogging in a one-horse gig' (Hanna and Danilo)

'Women, women, women' (Ensemble)

'Red as the rose in Maytime' (Valencienne and Camille)

'Quite à la mode Paree' (Hanna)

'There once were two royal children' (Danilo)

Act 3   'Eh voilà les belles Grisettes!' (Valencienne and Girls)

'Love unspoken' (Hanna and Danilo)

Der Graf von Luxemburg *(The Count of Luxembourg) by Franz Lehár, libretto by A. M. Wilner and Robert Bodanzky. First produced: Vienna, 1909; London 1911. New English version by Eric Maschwitz (1964). New version first produced Berlin, 1937. Set in pre-First World War Paris. (G.V.)*

Strangers interrupt a bohemian revel at the studio of Armand Brissard, asking to speak with his friend René, the Count of Luxembourg. They have a lucrative proposition for the young man who has dissipated his entire fortune trying to exist as an artist. The elderly Russian Prince Basil Basilovitch wishes to marry a well-known singer, Angèle Didier, but cannot do so because she is a commoner. If, for half a million francs, René will marry her first, thus making her Countess of Luxembourg, they can be divorced in three months and the Prince will be able to satisfy convention by taking a former Countess as bride. René amusedly agrees, accepting the additional conditions that he must not see his bride, even during the ceremony; that he must stay out of Paris for the stated three months; and, above all, that he is to claim no marriage rights.

Angèle is brought in. Shut off from each other's sight by an

47

easel and canvas, she and René are promptly married by one of the strangers, who is a notary. Their hands, however, are joined through a hole made in the canvas, and a mutual sympathy is transmitted. Then they part.

Three months later a party is taking place at Angèle's house to celebrate her retirement from the stage pending her imminent divorce and re-marriage. Armand's girl-friend Juliette, who, tired of waiting for his offer of marriage, had become companion to Angèle, recognises him amongst the guests and they are reconciled. Armand has been travelling abroad with René, who has also come to the party as 'Baron Revel', unaware that he is in the home of his own wife, or that it is his own wife with whom on their meeting he falls instantly in love. Prince Basil, however, seeing what is up, tries to forestall complications by immediately announcing his engagement to Angèle. The facts of the marriage of convenience are thus brought to light, there is mutual recognition, and René and Angèle leave the party together, to discuss their dilemma at a hotel. There they meet a strange old woman who proves to be the Princess Stasa Kokozoff, just arrived from Russia with an order from the Czar instructing Prince Basil to marry her. Arriving just then in pursuit of Angèle, the Prince is aghast but helpless. René pays him back his money, having come into timely repossession of his lost fortune, and is free to acknowledge Angèle as his own Countess of Luxembourg.

PRINCIPAL NUMBERS

Act 1　'Carnival' (Ensemble)
　　　　'Two millionaires on Rue d'Amour' (Juliette and Armand)
　　　　'The Luxembourgs can make it go' (René)
　　　　'I'm so in love' (Prince)
　　　　'Fancy free' (Angèle)

48

Zigeunerliebe *(Gypsy Love) by Franz Lehár, libretto by
A. M. Willner and Robert Bodanzky. First produced: Vienna,
1910; London, 1912. New English version by Philip Park
(1963). Set on the Hungarian-Rumanian border in contemporary times. (G.V.)*

Zorika Dragotin, a wealthy landowner's daughter, has
become engaged to a young neighbour, Jonel Bolescu, and
a celebration is in progress at her father's hunting lodge. The
romantic Zorika is not so enthusiastic about the match as her
father or her fiancé and is in very ready mood to listen to the
violin-playing and romantic story-telling of Jonel's gypsy
half-brother, Jozsi, who is jealous for her love. A local
superstition says that if on the night of her betrothal a girl
drinks from the river near by, she will learn her future.
Flinging away her fiancé's bouquet and refusing him the
traditional kiss of promise, Zorika slips away, drinks, and
falls asleep in a quiet place under the moon.

She dreams she elopes with Jozsi and finds herself at an
inn on the estate of Ilona von Körösháza, a rich neighbour
of the Dragotins. Ilona also is in pursuit of Jozsi, but the time
comes when he and Zorika, now disowned by her father,
stand side by side for their gypsy wedding. Only then does
Zorika learn from him that he is marrying her without love,
and she sees Ilona waiting mockingly for Jozsi to join her.

While Zorika is going through this dream-agony, her
fiancé, Jonel, finds her and tenderly watches her sleeping. He

49

knows that she thinks him unromantic, compared with the gypsy fiddler, but his love for her is genuine. Meanwhile the party goes on. Ilona von Körösháza, who is present, is charming all the men with her uninhibited personality and lively singing. She hints that, if she were asked to, she might well be persuaded to take a gypsy husband. Jozsi knows what she means, but his answer is that his tribe are about to leave the neighbourhood and nothing will prevent him from going with them. Roving, not matrimony, is the life for him. Thus, Zorika wakes to find her faithful Jonel waiting and to realise that her gypsy love, waking or sleeping, was all a dream.

PRINCIPAL NUMBERS

Act 1 'The wild bird' (Zorika)
     'The garden of love' (Zorika and Jozsi)
     'Cosmopolitan' (Ilona)
     'What I like about you' (Ilona and Dragotin)
Act 2 'Love and wine' (Andor)
     'A little maiden' (Zorika, Jozsi and Andor)
     'You're in love' (Ilona and Dragotin)
     'The best game' (Jonel and Kajetan)
     'I go so' (Ilona and Jozsi)
Act 3 'Home again' (Dragotin and Chorus)
     'Gypsy love' (Jozsi)

Frasquita *by Franz Lehár, libretto by A. M. Willner and Heinz Reichert. First produced: Vienna, 1922; London, 1925. Set in Spain and Paris in contemporary times. (J.W.)*

Aristide Girot is a French industrialist living in Spain with his daughter Dolly, who is to marry Girot's Parisian nephew

Armand Mirbeau, whom she has never met. Armand arrives, bringing with him Hippolyt Gallipot, an anthropologist friend, whom Dolly promptly mistakes for her fiancé. Armand, in any case, is quickly bewitched by Frasquita, a beautiful gypsy girl. Their association begins inauspiciously when he accuses her of stealing his cigarette case, but he is soon apologising and she is kissing him passionately. Actually, she is taking her revenge for the unfounded accusation, and, having stirred him to intense desire, she leaves him mockingly.

Later, in a night club, Armand and Frasquita come face to face again. She tells him condescendingly that he may approach her later bringing a mass of red roses; she will then consider whether to unbend to him; but, despite herself, she is attracted by him. He acquires the roses and serenades her.

Before the rendezvous can be kept, however, old Girot, full of champagne, steals the roses, hoping to gain Frasquita's favours for himself, but is mobbed by chorus girls who whirl him off into song and dance. Armand manages to acquire a further supply of flowers and is once more embarking upon his romantic quest when Dolly encounters him, thinks the roses are for her, and is affronted when Frasquita arrives and takes them. Frasquita again mocks Armand, handing back the roses to Dolly and telling him to stick to his fiancée; but she agrees to meet him later, after she has sung to a party of men in a private room. Incensed at being excluded, Armand breaks into the party, only to be told by Frasquita that she hates the sight of him. He leaves dejectedly and she bursts into tears – of love.

Totally neglected by Armand, Dolly marries Hippolyt. Back in Paris, they visit the pining American at his flat and then depart for the carnival, in which he has no wish to join. Old Girot also arrives, to ask Armand if he will lend him the flat for the evening to entertain a girl. Armand agrees and his uncle leaves to fetch the lady. But it is all an elaborate trick. When the door opens again, there stands Frasquita. She throws herself into Armand's arms, and Girot beams his blessing from the background.

PRINCIPAL NUMBERS

Act 1 'Tell me, what is love?' (Frasquita)
       'On every little leaf' (Frasquita)
Act 2 'The longing heart' (Armand and Frasquita)
       Serenade (Armand)
       'As young as you feel' (Girot)
Act 3 'Kiss me for ever' (Dolly and Hippolyt)

Paganini *by Franz Lehár, libretto by Paul Knepler and Bela Jenbach. First produced: Vienna, 1925; London 1937. English version by A. P. Herbert. Set in Italy, early 19th century. (G.V.)*

Nicolò Paganini, the virtuoso of the violin, is staying at a village near the town of Lucca, where his forthcoming recital is already sold out, when he meets the Princess Maria Anna Elisa, sister to Napoleon Bonaparte. Attracted first by his violin playing and then by his handsome looks, she intercedes for him with her husband, who disapproves of Paganini and has forbidden the concert to take place. The Prince is adamant, until his wife forces his hand with evidence of his association with Bella Giretti, prima ballerina of the Court Opera. Already in love with Anna Elisa, Paganini is only too happy to take up residence at her Court and suspend his concert touring, despite the pleas of his manager, Bartucci.

Court life stimulates Paganini's fondness for gambling. He loses heavily. When money runs out he stakes his precious violin – and loses it. Luckily, the winner is the Court Chamberlain, the Marchese Pimpinelli, who admires Bella Giretti but is unskilled in the art of wooing. For the return of his violin, Paganini gives him a lesson in love: 'Girls were made to love and kiss'.

But Paganini's own idyll is coming to an end. Word has reached Napoleon in Paris of his married sister's affair with the violinist. He sends an emissary, Count Hédouville, with an ultimatum to Paganini: either he leaves the state of Lucca or he will be arrested. Anna Elisa once more takes his part, until the jealous Bella Giretti shows her a love song composed by Paganini and dedicated to her. Anna Elisa abandons him to arrest; but only briefly. He gives a farewell recital and plays so brilliantly that she cannot let Count Hédouville take him. She leads Paganini to a carriage and gives orders for him to be carried safely across the frontier.

Paganini reaches a rough inn where low revels are in progress. He is soon followed by Bella Giretti, begging him to take her with him. He says he intends to change his ways and dedicate his life to his art. Bella decides to settle for Pimpinelli, and leaves. A girl street-singer comes in, recognisably Anna Elisa. But she has only come to take an oblique farewell of the artist whom she realises she has no right to keep from bestowing his great gift on the world at large.

PRINCIPAL NUMBERS

Act 1 'Napoleon Bonaparte' (Pimpinelli and Chorus)
      'Love live for ever' (Anna Elisa)
      'Beautiful Italy' (Paganini)
      'My faithful violin' (Anna Elisa and Paganini)

Der Zarewitsch *(The Czarevich) by Franz Lehár, libretto by Bela Janbech and Heinz Reichert, based on the play by Gabryela Zapolska. First produced: Berlin, 1927. English version by Adam Carstairs (1972). Set in St Petersburg and Naples, late 19th century. (G.V.)*

The Czarevich, heir to the Russian throne, has taste neither for regal pomp nor for the society of others, especially that of women. He prefers to keep to his own austere quarters, attended by his manservant, Ivan, and cultivate physical fitness. His uncle, the Grand Duke, wishing to change his attitude and prepare him for marriage, engages a dancer, Sonja, to visit the Czarevich in the guise of a young officer, make friends with him, and then reveal her sex; all in the hope that the heir will then find himself in love with her.

Sonja has to reveal her sex all too soon, for the Czarevich invites his visitor to join in his gymnastics and when she removes her tunic there is no denying her figure. She admits everything. Expecting the Grand Duke to have her punished for failing in her task, the Czarevich generously falls in with the plot and lets Sonja stay in his apartments. After a time, they find themselves in love.

The time is drawing nigh for the Czarevich to marry. The Grand Duke informs Sonja that she must now leave. When the Czarevich hears this he refuses a summons to attend the

Court to greet his official fiancée, Princess Militza; instead, he gives a party for Sonja and her dancer friends. The party is interrupted by the Grand Duke, who accuses him of putting his duty to his country second to his infatuation with a prostitute. The Czarevich hotly defends Sonja's reputation, while she says nothing. He agrees to obey the Czar's summons, but as soon as he and Sonja are left alone she confesses that she had merely been obeying orders, and is faithful only to him.

The Czarevich has defied his father after all and taken Sonja to live with him in Naples, where Ivan and his wife Mascha attend them. The Grand Duke turns up once more, with the news that the Czar is likely to die and that the heir must be at hand in Russia to assume the throne. The Czarevich refuses to leave Sonja. Again, the Grand Duke appeals to her for help. Despite her feelings, she pleads with the Czarevich to do his duty. He does not waver until a telegram is brought to say that the Czar is dead. Brought face to face with his destiny, the new Czar bids his love farewell for ever.

PRINCIPAL NUMBERS

Act 1 'Let me swing you gently' (Mascha and Ivan)
   'Someday I'll find him' (Sonja)
   'The Volga Song' (Czarevich)
   'There's nothing like champagne' (Sonja, Czarevich and Ivan)

Act 2 'Love is mine at last' (Sonja and Czarevich)
   'Napolitana (My love)' (Czarevich)
   'Love me now, kiss me now' (Sonja and Czarevich)
   'Late tonight I'll come back to you' (Mascha and Ivan)
   'Love today and cry tomorrow' (Sonja and Dancers)

Act 3 'Waves tossing lightly' (Sonja and Czarevich)
   'Kiss me!' (Sonja and Czarevich)

Friederike *(Frederica) by Franz Lehár, libretto by Ludwig Herzer and Fritz Löhner. First produced: Berlin, 1928; London, 1930. English version by Adrian Ross and Harry S. Pepper. Set in Sesenheim, in Alsace-Lorraine, and Strasbourg, in 1771 and 1779. (G.V.)*

Pastor Johann Jakob Brion of Sesenheim has two daughters – the mettlesome Salomea and the elder Friederike, who is of a quieter nature. When a crowd of students arrive in the little town one Whitsunday, Salomea joyfully joins in their singing and dances away with them; for among them is her sweetheart, Friederich Weylandt, a medical student. Friederike stays behind to wait for a solitary student, Johann Wolfgang Goethe, who is reading law but is a poet at heart. They are sincerely in love, and Friederike is thrilled to tell him that she and her sister have been asked to stay with their aunt and uncle in Strasbourg, so that in future they will be able to meet more often.

Friederike's Strasbourg aunt gives a party in Goethe's honour: he has been invited to become Poet Laureate to the Archduke of Saxe-Weimar. He sings of his love for Friederike – 'O maiden, my maiden!' The Archduke's tutor arrives to escort him to Weimar. When Goethe happens to ask why his predecessor, the famous Christoph Martin Wieland, vacated the post, he is told that the Archduke had come to feel that a Laureate with a wife and family was squandering his creative resources, and decided to appoint a bachelor instead. Goethe replies that he will not hear of giving up his Friederike. The Courtier's persuasions are in vain; but Weylandt, who has overheard the conversation, seeks out Friederike and assures her that she will only be inviting misery if she does not make Goethe take this great opportunity for his art's sake.

56

Sadly she agrees and tries to reason with Goethe. He will not listen to her, so she flirts with another student, making Goethe believe that her supposed love for him had been only a passing attraction. This cuts him to the heart. He informs the Courtier that he is ready to leave, and takes a cold farewell of a heartbroken Friederike.

Eight years later, back at Sesenheim, the Archduke, attended by the now-famous Goethe, visits Pastor Brion's rectory. Friederike, who has remained unmarried, is introduced, and the Archduke, asking about his Laureate's youth, learns the facts of her self-sacrifice. But it is too late to change anything. When the visit ends, Goethe and Friederike part again for ever.

PRINCIPAL NUMBERS

Act 1 'Little roses, little flowers' (Friederike)
      'Wonderful!' (Goethe)
      'My heart lies in your hand' (Friederike and Goethe)
      'Wayside Rose' (Goethe)
Act 2 'Maid of Alsace' (Salomea and Lenz)
      'All my yearning, all my loving' (Friederike and Goethe)
      'Oh maiden, my maiden!' (Goethe)
      'Why did you kiss my heart awake?' (Friederike)
Act 3 Rhineland Dance
      'A heart as pure as gold' (Goethe)

Das Land des Lächelns *(The Land of Smiles) by Franz Lehár, libretto by Ludwig Herzer and Fritz Löhner. First produced: Berlin, 1929; London, 1931. English version by Harry Graham ,and by Christopher Hassall (1959, Sadler's Wells). Set in Vienna and China in 1912. (G.V.)*

Count Gustav von Pottenstein, known as Gustl, is looking forward to marrying Lisa, daughter of the Viennese Count Lichtenfels. But he has an exotic rival, Prince Sou-Chong, a Chinese diplomat of great charm and wealth, who is deeply in love with Lisa. The Count is on Gustl's side; he wishes his daughter to marry one of her own race. However, when Sou-Chong is suddenly ordered to return to Peking to take up a ministerial post and asks her to go with him as his wife, Lisa knows that her heart will not let her refuse.

All goes well at first in Peking. The arrival of Gustl, as Military Attaché to the Austrian Embassy, presents no complications, since he has been much taken by Sou-Chong's young sister, Mi. In contrast to Mi, who emulates Western sophistication and dress, Sou-Chong adheres to Chinese tradition, to the extent of horrifying Lisa by telling her that he is required to maintain four Chinese wives in addition to her. Despite his assurances that it is purely a formality and they will be wives only in name, she refuses to accept the indignity. He reminds her sharply that he is her husband and therefore her master. She retorts that she detests him, and goes to Gustl for help in returning to her own country, for which, in any case, she is already homesick.

Sou-Chong has anticipated the move and has his palace doors locked before Gustl can escort Lisa out. Mi comes to their aid. She opens the temple door for them to leave. They find Sou-Chong facing them. His expression is ferocious, but when he speaks it is with all his customary tenderness towards

58

Lisa. He tells her she may go, if she must, and asks Gustl to look after her with all his care. For a moment the old love burns again in their gaze; then Lisa and Gustl go, leaving Mi weeping and Sou-Chong inscrutably expressionless.

PRINCIPAL NUMBERS

Act 1 'Waltz while you may' (Lisa and Chorus)
      'Patiently smiling' (Sou-Chong)
      'You're never too old' (Countess Roheim and Col. Block)
      'Lonely serenade' (Sou-Chong and Girls)
      'I have searched the earth' (Lisa and Sou-Chong)
Act 2 'Love! What has given you this magic power?' (Lisa, Sou-Chong and Chorus, Mi and Girls)
      'You are my heart's delight' (Sou-Chong)
      'My homeland' (Lisa and Chorus)
Act 3 'No other love' (Lisa, Gustl and Mi)

Schön ist die Welt *(So Fair the World) by Franz Lehár, libretto by Ludwig Herzer and Fritz Löhner (based on an earlier work* Endlich Allein*). First produced: Vienna, 1931. Set in the Swiss Alps in contemporary period. (G.V.)*

The Crown Prince Georg, accompanied by his father, the King of a European country, arrives at an Alpine resort to meet the Princess Elisabeth zu und von Lichtenberg, to whom he is to be married for the sake of his country's financial position. Neither had seen the other before, so that when Georg stopped his car *en route* to mend a puncture for a girl motorist they did not recognise each other as betrothed. They had, however, been mutually attracted, and Georg,

59

on arrival at the hotel, dumbfounds his father by announcing that he will not meet the expected princess, nor will he marry her; there are beautiful things in the world to be explored first.

Incognitos are being punctiliously observed by everyone at the hotel, so that Georg and Elisabeth remain unaware of each other's identity. They find they both love mountaineering and arrange to climb together the next day. After an early start they reach the summit of their mountain, where there is a well-equipped hut in which Elisabeth serves a meal and they listen to the radio together. An S.O.S. flash announces that the Princess zu und von Lichtenberg is missing from her hotel, and gives a description of her. Georg recognises his companion. She does not deny who she is, but before his identity can emerge they notice that the time of day and the weather have closed in on them. A thunderous avalanche near by frightens Elisabeth into Georg's arms. It is now too late to descend the mountain, so they spend the night where they are – she in the hut, he on a bench outside.

Next morning the pair return to the hotel, where everyone has reached a frenzy of anxiety. Only now, as Georg prepares to tell his father, the King, that he has found the woman he wishes to marry, is his identity revealed, and he has to admit that by climbing a mountain to get away from her, he has come to fall in love with the very girl he had refused to marry.

PRINCIPAL NUMBERS

Act 1   'So fair the world' (Georg)
        Tango: 'Rio de Janeiro' (King)
Act 2   'Believe me, I love you' (Georg)
        'How bright the sun' (Georg and Elisabeth)
Act 3   'I am loved!' (Elisabeth)

Giuditta *by Franz Lehár, libretto by Paul Knepler and Fritz Löhner. First produced: Vienna, 1934. English version by Adam Carstairs (1971). Set in a Mediterranean port, North Africa, and a European capital, in contemporary times. (G.V.)*

Giuditta is the beautiful young wife of a disgruntled working man, Manuel, from whom, despite his love for her and his hard work on her behalf, she longs to escape. The chance comes when she meets Captain Octavio, an officer about to embark for service in North Africa. They fall in love at once, and she sails with him.

After they have lived together for a short time in a North African garrison town, Giuditta and Octavio face the prospect of having to part, as his regiment is preparing to march against the Arabs. She begs him not to go. He hesitates, but the taunt of 'Deserter!' from his friend Lieutenant Antonio rallies him to duty and he leaves with his comrades.

Incensed at what she sees as his spurning of her love, Giuditta does not wait for Octavio to come back, but moves to a city, where her singing talent soon makes her the star of a night club. She is immensely popular, and attracts plenty of advances from rich men, among them an English nobleman, Lord Barrymore. One evening, after dining with him in a private room at the club, she leaves on his arm to go to his car. They pause while he fastens a superb necklace on her, then they go out. A witness of all this has been Octavio, no longer a soldier, but a broken man since the loss of Giuditta. He is tempted to run after them, but restrains himself, knowing she would spurn him.

Octavio pulls himself together to the extent of finding work as a pianist, playing at cabarets and special functions. One of his engagements is to play softly outside the hotel room of a wealthy Duke who is entertaining a woman. Seeing that she is Giuditta, Octavio plays a tune associated with their short-lived idyll. Giuditta is moved and begs Octavio to return to her. For all his unhappiness without her, he can only refuse: her love has been his curse. Giuditta leaves sadly with the Duke. Octavio, symbolically, closes the piano.

A sub-plot in the earlier scenes concerns the contrasting fortunes of Pierrino, a fruit-vendor, and Anita, a fisher-girl, both from Giuditta's town, who also make their way to North Africa in search of fortune, fail to find it, but fulfil their love there.

PRINCIPAL NUMBERS

Act 1 'Comrades, this life is the life for me!' (Octavio)
       'A sea of love enfolds me' (Giuditta)
Act 2 'When you're in love, you have bells in your heart' (Anita and Pierrino)
       'Blue as the summer sky above' (Giuditta and Octavio)
Act 3 'Love, gentle and tender' (Octavio)
Act 4 'My love, will you elope with me?' (Anita and Pierrino)
       'Kiss my lips and your heart is aflame' (Giuditta)
Act 5 'Love was a dream' (Octavio)

Frau Luna *(Castles in the Air) by Paul Lincke, libretto by H. Bolten-Baeckers. First produced: as one-act operetta, Berlin, May 1899; revised and extended version, Berlin, December 1899; London, 1911. Set in Berlin and on the Moon.*

Fritz Steppke, a young engineer, has built a balloon in which he and two friends, Lämmermeier and Pannecke, hope to reach the Moon, a project which finds no favour in the eyes of his landlady, Frau Pusbach, and her niece Marie, whom he is to marry. Troubled in his mind, Fritz lies down to sleep, and dreams. . . .

Lämmermeier and Pannecke, equipped for the flight, call for Fritz. The three elude Frau Pusbach across the rooftops, reach the balloon and cast off. The landlady scrambles aboard just as the balloon leaves the ground.

After an enchanting journey through space, the balloon reaches the Moon; but the welcome given to the Earth-travellers is not as warm as they might have wished. Theophilus, the head of the Moon-mechanics who keep its surface polished and its light bright, had visited Berlin during an eclipse and had an encounter with a woman at the zoo. He recognises Frau Pusbach as the woman and fears she will compromise him with Stella, maid to Frau Luna, the Moon Queen. He orders the travellers' arrest. Frau Pusbach threatens him with the consequence of their being convicted, but they have to stand trial, thinking wistfully of the comparative delights of Berlin.

Frau Luna hears from Stella of the astronauts' visit and summons them to her magnificent palace. Fritz attracts her immensely. She proceeds to set about his seduction, to the annoyance of Prince Sternschnuppe, the owner of a space-ship, who is visiting the Moon in yet another attempt to win Frau Luna. Theophilus suggests to the Prince that the best means of putting a stop to this will be to fetch Marie from Earth and confront Fritz with her. Prince Sternschnuppe takes his advice. On the very point of surrendering to Frau Luna's magic charms, Fritz sees his Earth-sweetheart and goes to her. Frau Luna, touched, relinquishes him and accepts the Prince, who is only too delighted to give the Berliners an immediate lift home.

'What can equal the beauty of Spring' (Ensemble)
'O, Theophilus!' (Frau Luna)
'Bestow on me a little love' (Prince and Frau Luna)
'Castles in the Moon' (Frau Luna)
'Trust a fellow from Berlin!' (Theophilus)
'From the stars' (Frau Luna)
'The Berlin air' (Ensemble)

Les P'tites Michu *(The Little Michus) by André Messager, libretto by Albert van Loo and Georges Duval. First produced: Paris, 1897; London, 1905. English version by Henry Hamilton. Set in Paris in 1810.*

The girl pupils of Mademoiselle Herpin's school are playing at Blind Man's Buff, and one of them, Blanche-Marie Michu, has just incurred a forfeit. The girls sentence her to kiss the first person to come into the garden. It proves to be no hardship, for in strides a handsome Captain of Hussars, Gaston Rigaud, Mademoiselle Herpin's gallant nephew, who enthusiastically kisses both Blanche-Marie and her twin sister Marie-Blanche.

The next arrivals are Monsieur Michu, a Parisian pastry-cook, his wife, and their assistant, Aristide, for whom Marie-Blanche nurtures a schoolgirl love. The Michus are the parents of only one of the 'twins', and do not know which; for, seventeen years earlier, they had been entrusted with the care of the new-born baby daughter of the widowed Marquis des Ifs, who was fleeing from arrest, and had soon afterwards mixed her up with their own new baby. Not knowing which was which, they have brought up the girls as their own twins and lived in hope that the Marquis might never return to claim his child. The girls are inseparable friends.

The dreaded time, however, is nigh. A Private Bagnolet arrives with orders from the Marquis to bring his daughter to his Paris house. Unable to make head or tail of the Michus' attempts to explain the position, Bagnolet carries off the lot of them to his master in military style.

When they reach the Marquis's house they find the handsome Captain Rigaud there. He saved the Marquis's life in the field and has been promised his daughter's hand in consequence. When it proves impossible to decide which of the girls is his daughter, the Marquis makes the arbitrary choice of Marie-Blanche, whom the Michus must henceforward bring up as the Captain's betrothed. Marie-Blanche is pleased enough to begin with, but soon realises that her true love is still Aristide, while Blanche-Marie yearns for the Captain. Marie-Blanche settles the matter for both of them. Finding a dress that had belonged to the late Marquise, she dresses Blanche-Marie in it, arranges her hair in the style shown in a portrait of the Marquise, and presents her 'twin' to the Marquis. He is so struck by the likeness to his beloved wife that he happily agrees to the girls' request to change places, and accepts Blanche-Marie as his daughter. Captain Rigaud and Aristide comply willingly, and take the girls off together to the altar.

PRINCIPAL NUMBERS

Act 1 'Two little maids' (Marie-Blanche and Blanche-Marie)
'Oh many a gallant corps today' (Gaston)
'Our Fairy Godmamma is here' (Aristide)
Act 2 'St Valentine' (Marie-Blanche and Blanche-Marie)

Véronique *by André Messager, libretto by Albert van Loo and Georges Duval. First produced: Paris, 1898; London, 1903. English version by Henry Hamilton. Set in Paris in 1840.*

Hélène de Solanges and her Aunt Ermerance, attended by their groom Seraphin, come to Coquenard's flower-shop in Paris to order blooms for that evening, when Hélène is to be married to Count Florestan de Valaincourt. The marriage is to take place in the presence of the King, who has ordered it for the benefit of the Count, who will be imprisoned for debt if he does not marry money quickly; but although Hélène has seen him, Florestan has never met her, and when she sees him approaching the flower-shop she and her aunt hide to find out the reason for his visit. He has come to bid farewell to the florist's wife, Agatha, who has been his mistress, and they hear him tell her how he dislikes having to marry what he expects will turn out to be a dowdy little bride. He invites all the girl shop assistants to his last party as a bachelor and leaves. The furious Hélène bribes one of the girls to find work dresses for herself and her aunt and gets Coquenard, who is at once much taken with Aunt Ermerance, to engage them, giving their names as Véronique and Estelle respectively.

Thus they are able to attend Florestan's party at a woodland restaurant. Florestan is stricken by the beauty of 'Véronique' and woos her earnestly, first on a donkey ride and then on a swing – 'Swing high, swing low' – but she slips away when he becomes too ardent. He tries to prevent her getting back to Paris without him by dismissing all the carriages, but she outwits him by bribing her coachman's bride, who has just been celebrating her wedding, to lend her her veil and let her get away in the bridal carriage.

Florestan declares that, after the beautiful Véronique, he cannot bear the thought of his plain bride-to-be and says he will go to prison rather than marry. He is persuaded to bow to the inevitable and returns to Paris with a heavy heart. Arriving at the Tuileries to await his bride, he is astonished to find Véronique in Court dress, and even more amazed to learn that she is the woman he is having to marry. Humiliated by her knowledge that he had only that afternoon been chasing after a supposed shop-assistant, he maintains that he cannot possibly go through with the marriage. His little act of revenge upon Hélène works. She is dismayed; but he takes her in his arms and makes his true feelings for her plain.

PRINCIPAL NUMBERS

Act 1 'Out in the breezy morning air' (Hélène, Ermerance and Seraphin)
  'Life is short, my dear friends' (Florestan)
  'Take Estelle and Véronique' (Hélène)
Act 2 'Trot here, trot there' ('Swing high, swing low') (Florestan)
  'At weddings, as a general rule' (Seraphin and Chorus)
  'The bloom of an apple tree' (Agatha)
  'You've a charming little maiden' (Florestan)
  Letter Song (Florestan)
Act 3 'The garden of love' (Ermerance)
  'While I am waiting' (Hélène)

Monsieur Beaucaire *by André Messager, libretto by Frederick Lonsdale and Adrian Ross based on the novel by Booth Tarkington. First produced: Birmingham, 1919; London, 1919. Set in Bath, England, early in the 18th century.*

Having being committed to prison by his King, Louis XV of France, for refusing a royal command to marry, the Duc d'Orléans has escaped to England disguised as Monsieur Beaucaire, barber to the French Ambassador. He has come to the fashionable spa of Bath to look for the woman with whom he is in love, Lady Mary Carlisle, only to discover that his rival for her is the Duke of Winterset, who needs her large fortune to make up for the loss of his own. The Duke humiliates Beaucaire by having him turned out of the Pump Room because of his supposedly menial rank, but Beaucaire gets his revenge by catching Winterset cheating at cards and, for the price of his silence, makes him reintroduce him into society under a new identity at a ball given at Lady Rellerton's home, at which Lady Mary Carlisle is a guest.

Under the alias of 'Duc de Chateaurien', Beaucaire is introduced to Lady Mary and gets her to promise to present him with the rose from her hair. But the Duke of Winterset has not finished with him. He has paid a disreputable officer to insult his rival and challenge him to a duel. The fight takes place outside the ballroom, while the guests, in ignorance, continue to dance. At length, it is Beaucaire who re-enters victorious and claims his rose.

Some weeks later, at a garden party, the Duke of Winterset tries yet again: more desperately this time, for the romance between the French 'duke' and Lady Mary is the talk of Bath. Beaucaire is attacked by Winterset's friends. He fights them off, but is wounded and nearly overcome. As a final thrust, Winterset breaks his word and reveals that the so-called Duc de Chateaurien is only Beaucaire, the barber, who has deceived Lady Mary with his charms. Lady Mary turns away from Beaucaire and soon agrees to become Winterset's duchess, in gratitude for having been saved from an impostor. Beaucaire's unmasking, however, does not prevent his turning up at a function at the Pump Room in honour of the French Ambassador. Winterset's cronies attack him again, but this time he defends himself more successfully. Winterset is about to lead Lady Mary away from his odious presence, when the Ambassador enters. To general astonishment, the Ambassador greets Beaucaire as 'mon Prince' and reveals his true identity as cousin to the King of France. Winterset is denounced as a cheat and a schemer, and Lady Mary returns to the side of 'Monsieur Beaucaire'.

A sub-plot concerns a mercurial romance between Beaucaire's friend Molyneux and his fiancée Lucy.

PRINCIPAL NUMBERS

Prologue	'Red rose' (Beaucaire)
Act 1	'A little more' (Lucy and Molyneux)
	'I do not know' (Lady Mary)
	'English maids' (Beaucaire)
	'Lightly, lightly' (Lady Mary and Beaucaire)
Act 2	'When I was king of Bath' (Beau Nash)
	'That's a woman's way' (Lady Mary)
	'Philomel' (Lady Mary and Chorus)
	'Honour and love' (Molyneux)
	'Say no more' (Lady Mary and Beaucaire)
Act 3	'We are not speaking now' (Molyneux and Lucy)
	'A son of France' (Ambassador)

Der Bettelstudent *(The Beggar Student) by Karl Millöcker, libretto by 'F. Zell' (Camillo Walzel) and Richard Genée. First produced: Vienna, 1882; London, 1884. Revised versions by Gustav Quedenfeldt, Richard Bärs and Oskar Stalla, and by Christopher Hassall. Set in Cracow, Poland, 1704. (J.W).*

Colonel Ollendorf, German governor of the occupied Polish capital, is burning for revenge on a Polish girl, Laura Nowalska, who has slapped his face for kissing her in public, and on her noble but impoverished mother for referring to him in mocking terms. He offers freedom to a handsome young student, held prisoner in the city gaol, if he will pose as a millionaire prince and persuade the girl to marry him, so giving her and her mother a cruel awakening when they subsequently learn the truth. The student, Symon Symanowicz, agrees, on condition that his closest friend, Jan Janicki, may go free with him, impersonating his secretary.

The Colonel duly introduces the pair to Countess Nowalska and her daughters, Laura and Bronislawa. Symon and Laura fall in love at once; Symon is accepted without hesitation and the wedding day is fixed. The vengeful Colonel Ollendorf's plan seems to have worked perfectly.

The wedding day, a week later, finds Symon uneasy. He really loves Laura and cannot carry on with the deception, as he tries to tell his friend Jan, who has become attracted to Bronislawa Nowalska. Jan has more important things than romance on his mind at the moment. He reveals that he is really Count Opalinski, an aide-de-camp to the King of Poland, whose nephew, Duke Casimir, is in Cracow and only needs two hundred thousand crowns before he can mount the revolt that will drive the Germans from their city. Colonel Ollendorf has also heard of Jan's true identity, and comes to him with a proposition: if he will betray the Duke Casimir, he shall have a large reward. Jan stipulates two hundred thousand crowns and agrees.

Symon goes through with his wedding to Laura, and the Colonel is able to crow over having tricked her into marrying a penniless gaolbird. Bitterly hurt and humiliated, she leaves Symon.

Jan tells Symon how he has raised the money Duke Casimir needs, but that he must seem to honour his bargain and produce the 'Duke' for Ollendorf to arrest, pending the successful uprising. He asks Symon to assume the role, for his country's sake. Symon agrees and is arrested by Ollendorf. The Countess Nowalska and Laura are delighted to hear that the 'beggar student' was a duke in disguise, but this illusion also is shattered when gunfire is heard and word arrives that the real Duke Casimir has seized control of the city. The news of freedom from the German yoke, however, is enough to soften hard feelings, Colonel Ollendorf surrenders his office, and Laura happily accepts Symon in his own right.

PRINCIPAL NUMBERS

Act 1	'Bowing, smiling' (Ollendorf)
	'Let it go, let it pass' (Symon, Jan and Officers)
	'His Highness Malatesta' (Ensemble)
Act 2	'Lover mine' (Jan and Bronislawa)
	'What if?' (Symon, Laura and Chorus)
	'Ratpattapat!' (Ensemble)
Act 3	'I don't care' (Symon and Jan)

Die Dubarry *(The Dubarry) by Karl Millöcker, arranged by Theo Mackeben, libretto by Paul Knepler, J. M. Welleminsky and Hans Martin Cremer. First produced: Berlin, 1931; London, 1932. English version by Rowland Leigh and Desmond Carter. (A revised version of the original* Gräfin Dubarry *by Millöcker, with libretto by 'F. Zell' and Richard Genée, first produced in Vienna, 1879.) Set in Paris in the first half of the 18th century.*

Jeanne Beçu, an assistant in Madame Labille's millinery shop, has a rendezvous in a pleasure garden with a new admirer, the young painter René Lavallery. Their meeting is watched by the Count Dubarry, who is scheming to further his political ambitions by finding a young successor to the ageing Madame Pompadour as mistress for King Louis XV. Jeanne goes to live with Rene in his studio, where Dubarry visits her with his proposition. She refuses, and he goes, leaving some money behind in the hope that she will change her mind. René hears of the Count's visit, finds the money, and suspects the worst. He turns Jeanne out.

Jeanne makes a new career as a night-club singer and dancer, under the name Manon Rançon. Men vie with one another for her favours and one presses upon her a large sum of money, which she promptly loses at the gambling tables. Count Dubarry calms the angry man, pays him back, and escorts Jeanne away to his palace, where he proceeds to have her transformed into a lady and married, for convention's sake, to his brother. She despises Dubarry's scheme to use her to sway the King's interest away from the Countess de Grammont, who is supported by a rival political clique for the position of Royal mistress. She goes with Dubarry to a soirée given by the Princess of Luxembourg, who also thinks her the best choice for the King. René is at the soireé and Jeanne's love for him immediately revives; but she hears that it is a portrait of her by René that had awakened the King's interest, and thinks René had provided it to further his own ends. She turns away from him and willingly accompanies a courtier who has come to escort her to the King.

Louis XV is captivated by Jeanne, now officially Countess Dubarry, and makes her his favourite. Dubarry's political rival, the Duc de Choiseul, makes one last effort on behalf of the Countess de Grammont, who is his sister, by persuading the King to eavesdrop at a meeting between Jeanne and René. But all they hear is Jeanne finally rejecting the artist because she is sincerely in love with the King. Louis dismisses Choiseul from his court and proclaims the Countess Dubarry next in precedence to the throne.

PRINCIPAL NUMBERS

Act 1 'Without your love' (René and Jeanne)
'If I am dreaming' (René)
'Happy little Jeanne' (Jeanne)
'I give my heart' (Jeanne)
Act 2 'The road to happiness' (René and Jeanne)
'The Dubarry' (Jeanne and Chorus)

Orphée aux Enfers *(Orpheus in the Underworld) by Jacques Offenbach, libretto by Hector Crémieux. First produced: Paris, 1858; London, 1865. English versions by Geoffrey Dunn; Philip Park and Ronald Hanmer (1966). Set in mythological times.*

Orpheus and Eurydice are jaded with marriage. He bores her with his insistent violin playing despite her protests, while he resents her obvious love for a beekeeper, Aristaeus, which is offensive to public opinion and thus deleterious to his standing as Principal of the Thebes Academy of Music. Orpheus plants poisonous snakes around Aristaeus' dwelling as a deterrent; unfortunately it is Eurydice who is bitten and dies, and Aristaeus, revealing himself to be Pluto, King of the Underworld, carries her off to his domain. Orpheus is delighted, but outraged Public Opinion appears in person, to insist on escorting him to Mount Olympus to ask Jupiter, father of the Gods, to retrieve Eurydice. Orpheus reluctantly obeys, seen off by his child pupils who accompany their farewells excruciatingly on their violins.

Jupiter is in trouble from Diana, the huntress, for meddling with her *affaire* with Actaeon, besides being under criticism from the other gods for his own amorous record. To Orpheus' regret, he readily agrees to accompany him to the Underworld to demand Eurydice back. The other gods and goddesses, fancying an outing, insist on accompanying them and they all set off strap-hanging in an omnibus.

Eurydice in Pluto's apartments is guarded by the bibulous John Styx, who spends his time trying to gain her affections, insisting that his only drink is Lethe water, which makes him forgetful, and reminiscing about the days on Earth when he was King of the Boeotians. When the gods are heard approaching he hastily locks her in an adjoining room. Pluto denies that she is on the premises, or that he ever carried her off. Jupiter insists that Pluto stand trial before the Judges of the Underworld, but the court proceedings are reduced to chaos when a defence witness, the three-headed dog Cerberus, bites Jupiter. Cupid appears to Jupiter and offers to find Eurydice for him, which he soon does. Jupiter gleefully changes himself into a gilded fly and flits into the next room by way of the keyhole. He greatly

74

likes what he finds, and Eurydice in turn admires him. He throws off his disguise and they make plans to escape together during a grand bacchanalian revel which is to be held that evening. He changes her into a Bacchante, and their chance to leave occurs during the excitement of the famous Galop, or can-can; but Pluto has recognised her while she was singing and forestalls them with the reminder that Eurydice is the wife of Orpheus, whom she had quite overlooked. Orpheus enters, playing his eternal violin. Jupiter declares that Eurydice will be restored to him on Earth if Orpheus will head the procession back and not turn round until they have left Hades. Orpheus having agreed and set off, Jupiter startles him with a thunderbolt so that he spins round involuntarily. Thus he is freed from Eurydice and she from him, while the amorous Jupiter is once again triumphant.

PRINCIPAL NUMBERS

Act 1	'Shepherd boys and shepherdesses' (Chorus)
	'You've gone too far' (Orpheus and Eurydice)
	'My name is Aristaeus' (Aristaeus)
	'My death appears divinely smiling' (Eurydice)
	'Goodbye, Maestro dear' (Orpheus and Pupils)
Act 2	'Your conduct is erratic' (Ensemble)
	'Down to Hell' (Jupiter and Chorus)
Act 3	'When Pluto enthralled me with passion' (Eurydice)
	'When I was king of the Boeotians' (John Styx)
	'I'm Cerberus the triple-headed' (Cerberus)
	'What a pretty thing!' (Eurydice)
	'Hail, Pluto!' (Chorus)
	'Great god of wine, Evoe' (Chorus)

La Belle Hélène *(The Lovely Helen) by Jacques Offenbach, libretto by Henri Meilhac and Ludovic Halévy. First produced: Paris, 1864; London, 1866 as* Helen or Taken from the Greek, *adapted by F. C. Burnand. English versions by Geoffrey Dunn, Philip Park and Ronald Hanmer (1961). Set in Greece in mythological times.*

Hélène, consort of King Menelaus of Sparta, joins the worshippers before the Temple of Jupiter on the day of the Feast of Adonis, and entertains them with a paean of praise for Venus. Into their midst comes a shepherd, just back from Mount Ida where he has been watching Paris, son of King Priam of Troy, judging a beauty contest. The three contestants were all goddesses – Juno, Minerva and Venus – and Paris had declared the last the winner. In gratitude, she granted him the love of the supreme beauty, Hélène, who, by now, has fallen in love with the shepherd relating these events.

Enter now the Homeric Kings of Greece, and an intelligence contest follows which the shepherd takes part in – and wins outright! Revealing himself to be Paris, he suggests to the High Priest Calchas that it would be diplomatic if Hélène's husband were to absent himself for a time. After an oracular thunderclap, Calchas obligingly announces that, by decree of the Father of the Gods, King Menelaus must leave at once for a month in Crete.

Though Hélène is gratified by the turn of events, her wifely conscience is troubled. She succeeds in keeping Paris at bay, while seeking the counsel of Venus. Paris again seeks more practical aid from Calchas, who once again proves resourceful, praying to the gods in Hélène's hearing that, since she cannot cope with Paris literally in the flesh, they should send him to her in a dream. She falls asleep, to awake in Paris's arms, unaware that he is no dream-lover. But her procrastinations have consumed too much time: at this moment Menelaus returns, to surprise the pair in full duet.

Hélène insists to all and sundry that she has only been dreaming. Meanwhile, divorce has run rife throughout Sparta, and Calchas attributes this to Venus's annoyance that a love-match ordered by her has been blocked by Menelaus. The other kings urge Menelaus to relent and let his wife embrace her lover for the good of the state. Menelaus appeals to Venus to send her Grand Augur to settle the matter. This dignitary arrives and orders Hélène to take ship with him to Cythera, where she must appease Diana by sacrificing a herd of cattle. Reluctantly, Hélène goes aboard. But as soon as the anchor is weighed the Grand Augur reveals that he is Paris. Hélène is overjoyed; Menelaus, stranded and furious. The galley heads for Troy and all is set for the Trojan War.

PRINCIPAL NUMBERS

Act 1   'Immortal Jupiter!' (Chorus)
        'It's considered a moral duty' (Calchas)
        'For burning love and breathless rapture' (Hélène)
        The Judgement of Paris (Paris)

Act 2   'We all begin by truly trying' (Hélène)
        Dream duet (Paris and Hélène)
        'A husband who' (Hélène)

Act 3   'Venus has filled our hearts' (Chorus)
        'When all of Greece' (Menelaus, Agamemnon and
           Calchas)
        'Are you a Spartan madrigal society?' (Paris and
           Chorus)

La Vie Parisienne *by Jacques Offenbach, libretto by Henri Meilhac and Ludovic Halévy. First produced: Paris, 1866; London, 1872. English versions by Geoffrey Dunn; Philip Park and Ronald Hanmer (1967). Set in Paris in the 1850s.*

On a platform of the Gare de l'Ouest two young men-about-town, Gardefeu and Bobinet, await the train bringing the beautiful Metella, for whose favours they are rivals. When she arrives it is with another escort. Wandering disappointedly away, Gardefeu meets his former valet, Joseph, now a tourist courier, on his way to meet a rich Swedish couple, Baron and Baroness Gondremarck. Gardefeu fancies his chances with a baroness and pays Joseph to let him take his place. He escorts the couple to his own house, which he tells them is an annexe of the Grand Hotel. The Baron insists that rather than eat in the privacy of their room, he wants to see something of Paris life in the restaurant, so Gardefeu has to muster a crowd of pseudo-diners to fill the place, which he manages through his shoemaker, Frick, and Gabrielle, a glovemaker. Their friends make the dinner a gay and noisy success, at which Gabrielle pretends to be a colonel's widow.

Bobinet has by now approached Gardefeu with the proposition that they should offer the wealthy Baron a grand reception, which can be held in the sumptuous flat of Bobinet's noble aunt, who is away. Gardefeu sends the Baron alone, so that he himself can spend the evening with the Baroness. Once again the improvised entertainment goes with a tremendous swing, Bobinet attending in uniform as 'Admiral Walter of the Swiss Navy', the supposed owner of the apartment. His aunt's servants, dressed as members of high society, are the other 'guests', and Baron Gondremarck is more than a little taken with Admiral Walter's wife, actually Pauline, the parlourmaid.

Baron Gondremarck had brought with him to Paris an introduction to the same Metella who had disappointed Gardefeu and Bobinet at the railway station, and Gardefeu has undertaken to arrange a *tête-à-tête*. This takes place at the Café Anglais, noted for its gay parties, but Metella does not arrive alone. She tells the Baron that she has decided to return to her young admirer, Gardefeu, and has brought another girl for him to entertain in her place. The heavily veiled substitute turns out to be the Baroness.

Furious at Gardefeu's trickery, every detail of which he has by now discovered, the Baron bursts into a party at the same restaurant where Gardefeu is a guest and challenges him to a duel. He is reminded that, however much he may have been deceived, he has had a thoroughly good time in Paris for his money. The Baron has to admit the truth of it and everyone finishes up friends, with the party once more in full flow.

PRINCIPAL NUMBERS

Act 1   'Well isn't that just life' (Bobinet and Gardefeu)
'I'm the guide for every tourist' (Gardefeu)
'I'm a native of Brazil' (Matadores)
'Paree, Paree!' (Chorus)
Letter Song (Metella)

Act 2   'They say that true love is a ladder for scaling' (Pauline and Baron)
'Does he know he's splitting down the back?' (Ensemble)
'Nobody would call me a rover' (Bobinet and Ensemble)
'I'm a colonel's widow' (Gabrielle)

La Grande-Duchesse de Gérolstein *(The Grand Duchess of Gérolstein) by Jacques Offenbach, libretto by Henri Meilhac and Ludovic Halévy. First produced: Paris, 1867; London, 1867. English versions by Charles Lamb Kenney; Philip Park, John Grimsey and Ronald Hanmer (1969). Set in contemporary Central Europe.*

The Grand Duchess, ruler of the mid-European state of Gérolstein, is inspecting her troops before they march to war against a neighbouring state. Impressed by the physical attributes of one Private Fritz, she promotes him, in quick succession, to corporal, lieutenant and captain, to the annoyance of his commanding officer, General Boum, who is already jealous of Fritz over a peasant girl, Wanda. The son of a neighbouring ruler, Prince Paul of Steis-Stein-Steis-Laper-Bottmoll-Schorstenburg, whom the Court Chamberlain, Baron Puck, wishes to make the Grand Duchess's husband, arrives for a war conference, at which General Boum outlines his plan of attack. The General's strategy strikes Fritz as so inept that he interrupts and is invited by the Grand Duchess to join in the discussion. General Boum objects to a junior officer of common birth being admitted, so the Grand Duchess promotes Fritz to General and makes him Commander-in-Chief, with the title of Baron de Vermont-von-bock-bier. She also hands him the sword which her own father had always worn in battle, and General Fritz proudly leads her army away to war.

In due course he leads it victoriously back again and recounts his achievements to the Grand Duchess. Since he

1. *The Chocolate Soldier*. Constance Drever and C. H. Workman as Nadina and Bumerli. Lyric Theatre, 1910.

2. *Gypsy Love*. Sari Petrass and Robert Michaelis as Ilona and Jozsi. Daly's Theatre, 1912.

3. *Véronique*. Ruth Vincent and Lawrence Rea as Hélène and Florestan. Apollo Theatre, 1904.

4. *The Dollar Princess*. Lily Elsie and Joseph Coyne as Alice and her father. Daly's Theatre, 1909.

5. *A Waltz Dream*. Lily Elsie as Franzi. Daly's Theatre, 1911.

6. *The Merry Widow*. Lily Elsie and Joseph Coyne as Sonia (Hanna Glawari) and Danilo. Both are in national dress as worn during Act 2. Daly's Theatre, 1907.

7. *The Count of Luxembourg.* Bertram Wallis and Lily Elsie as René and
Angèle. Daly's Theatre, 1911.

9. *Die Fledermaus*. Catherine Wilson and Émile Belcourt as Rosalinda and Eisenstein. Sadler's Wells Opera Company, London Coliseum, 1971.

8. (left) *The Little Michus*. Mabel Green and Adrienne Augarde as Marie-Blanche and Blanche-Marie. Daly's Theatre, 1905.

10. *La Vie Parisienne*. Suzanne Steele as Metella. Sadler's Wells Theatre, 1961.

11. *Orpheus in the Underworld.* June Bronhill and Kevin Miller as Eurydice and Orpheus. Sadler's Wells Theatre, 1960.

12. *The Dubarry*. Lawrence Anderson and Anny Ahlers as Louis XV and Jeanne. His Majesty's Theatre, 1932.

13. *Madame Pompadour*. Evelyn Laye in the title role. Daly's Theatre, 1923.

14. *The Grand Duchess of Gérolstein.* Julia Matthews in the title role. Covent Garden, 1867.

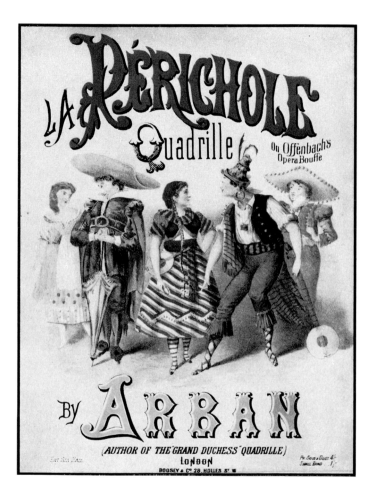

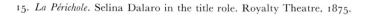

15. *La Périchole*. Selina Dalaro in the title role. Royalty Theatre, 1875.

16. *Lilac Time*. Richard Tauber (centre) as Schubert, and the 'Four jolly brothers'. Viennese Opera Company production. Aldwych Theatre, 1933.

cannot see for himself that she loves him, she declares herself obliquely, but he is still uncomprehending and infuriates her by asking permission to marry Wanda. The Grand Duchess throws in her lot with General Boum, Baron Puck and Prince Paul, who plan to assassinate Fritz.

Before the murder can take place, Baron Grog, an emissary from Prince Paul's father, arrives to try to persuade the Grand Duchess to marry Paul. She is more taken with Grog himself, and loses interest in the plot against Fritz. When General Boum protests at her withdrawal, she orders him to meet Fritz in single combat instead. The General has to agree, but he fails to turn up for the duel. This gives Baron Puck an idea to enhance Prince Paul in the Grand Duchess's eyes. He pays Fritz to pretend that he has been waylaid by a masked man, that they have fought together, and that the masked man has won. The impressionable Duchess will be full of curiosity to meet anyone man enough to defeat the heroic Fritz, and Paul will be produced as the victorious stranger.

Fritz agrees and presents himself, shamefaced and dishevelled, to the Grand Duchess. She strips him of his title and honours and bestows them on Baron Grog. When he tells her how proud his wife and six children will be of him, she promptly relieves him of them again. Baron Puck produces the masked stranger. The admiring Grand Duchess offers her hand in marriage. When the stranger is revealed as Prince Paul, she keeps her promise and they join Fritz and Wanda in a double wedding ceremony.

PRINCIPAL NUMBERS

Act 1 'Piff, Paff, Pouff!' (Boum)
Song of the Regiment (Grand Duchess, Fritz and Chorus)
Song of the Sword (Grand Duchess)

La Périchole *by Jacques Offenbach, libretto by Henri Meilhac and Ludovic Halévy. First produced: Paris, 1868; London, 1870. English versions by M. Valency; Philip Park, John Grimsey and Ronald Hanmer (1973). Set in Peru in contemporary period.*

Two wandering singers, Piquillo and La Périchole, arrive outside the Three Cousins tavern in Lima, to find a crowd celebrating the birthday of their Viceroy, Don Andrès de Ribiera. They entertain the revellers, hoping to earn enough for their wedding fees, but the crowd are more interested in some acrobats and a pack of performing dogs, whom they try to follow, leaving the square empty. Piquillo goes off to try another part of the town, leaving the exhausted Périchole to sleep. The Viceroy, whose idea of enjoyment is to wander the town incognito, comes upon her and offers her a meal. She hesitates, but he discloses his identity and offers her a place at Court. Too poor and hungry to refuse, she writes an explanatory note to leave for Piquillo.

A law stipulates that single women may not live within the Palace precincts, and the Viceroy's notion of circumventing this is to procure a man to marry La Périchole and then make himself scarce. The man the Viceroy's emissaries happen to choose is Piquillo. Périchole sees this and is overjoyed, but Piquillo is made so drunk by the courtier persuading him to go through with the marriage that he has no idea who is beside him at the altar.

Next day, Piquillo, now the bearer of a noble title, asks for his fee and permission to leave. He is reminded of one remaining duty: to hand over his wife to the Viceroy. He is willing enough to comply with this, until he discovers that it is his own Périchole that he is surrendering. He denounces her for having helped to trick him. She retorts with a withering commentary upon men in general. Piquillo persists and succeeds in offending the Viceroy, who has him thrown into prison.

Périchole visits Piquillo in his cell and persuades him of her innocence. They try to bribe the gaoler, but he turns out to be the Viceroy, enjoying yet another role in disguise. He has them chained to opposite walls and leaves them, telling Périchole that she will be freed when she consents to yield to him. When he has gone, part of the wall slides back and a veteran prisoner, the Marquis de Santarem, enters from his cell by a passage which he has taken twelve years to construct. He releases the young couple. The Viceroy returns and the three overpower him and tie him up.

The escapers make their way to the Three Cousins. They are soon traced there by the Viceroy and his lieutenants, who threaten to flog the proprietors for sheltering the fugitives. The latter come out of hiding and plead for pardon. Moved by the sight of the young lovers, the Viceroy consents and forgiveness reigns all round.

PRINCIPAL NUMBERS

Act 1 'The Three Cousins' (Anita, Berginella and Manuelita)

'Incognito' (Viceroy)

'She was so brave' (Périchole and Piquillo)

Letter Song (Périchole)

'That glass of wine' (Périchole)

La Fille du Tambour-Major *(The Drum-Major's Daughter) by Jacques Offenbach, libretto by Alfred Duru and Henri Chivot. English version by H. B. Farnie. First produced: Paris, 1879; London, 1880. Set in Lombardy in 1806.*

Lombardy is under Austrian domination, but relief appears to be imminent, for Napoleon's troops have crossed the Alps and are spreading rapidly into Italy, welcomed and assisted by Italian patriots. Seemingly detached from these events lives a community of girls in a convent school, whose concern is more for their Saint's Day holiday than for political upheaval. One of their number, Stella, is an exception. The news that French soldiers are in the vinicity excites her so much that she sings a patriotic song, for which the Mother Prioress packs her off into solitary confinement. The consequence is that when the troops are actually heard approaching, and the nuns hurry their pupils away to a near-by convent, Stella is left behind. Her alarm when the invaders arrive and find her is short-lived, for their leader, Lieutenant Robert, is notably handsome and the elderly Drum-Major, Monthabor, is kindly. Also in the party are Claudine, a camp follower whose love for the Lieutenant is not returned, and Griolet, a drummer, who, in turn, loves Claudine but is snubbed by her.

84

The soldiers are followed by Stella's father, the Duke Della Volta, bringing with him an old nobleman, Bambini, with the idea of marrying him off to the girl in settlement of a financial embarrassment. Against her will, but to the relief of Claudine, who is already jealous of her, Stella is taken away from her soldier friends. However, she refuses to marry Bambini and is soon reunited with the soldiers when they arrive at her father's château with an order requiring them to be billeted there. It is not the only reunion: Drum-Major Monthabor and Stella's mother recognise one another as former husband and wife, from the days when the Duchess Della Volta had been a laundress. It soon emerges that Stella is their daughter. Openly declaring her love for Lieutenant Robert, she enlists herself as a Vivandière and leaves with the soldiers, despite an attempt by her father and his friends to prevent her by force.

Lieutenant Robert and Claudine become separated from the others in leaving the château. After adventures on the road, all find themselves in Milan, hiding at separate addresses. The Duke arrives, seeking Stella, but does not recognise her dressed as a coachman. In her over-confidence she unwittingly tells him the address where Robert is in hiding and the lieutenant is arrested. The Duke now sees a way to blackmail Stella into marrying old Bambini: Robert's freedom shall be her reward. Before long, the excited Bambini is standing beside his veiled bride at the church, but Robert, released and furious at the trick that has been played on his Stella, whips off her veil – to disclose Claudine, who, in league with the Duchess, had assumed the disguise to save Stella, even in the knowledge that it would mean delivering her into Robert's arms; which is precisely what happens.

Act 1   'Forbidden Fruit' (Stella)
      'Honour and Glory' (Robert and Chorus)
      'Italia, land of song' ⎫
      'Beyond the Hills'   ⎬ (Stella)
                        ⎭
      'The Princess and the Recruit' (Claudine and
         Griolet)
Act 2   'Stella!' (Chorus)
      'It must be now' (Stella and Robert)
Act 3   'By chance we had' – Tarantella (Robert, Claudine
         and Chorus)

Les Cloches de Corneville *(The Bells of Corneville) by Robert Planquette, libretto by 'Clairville' (L. F. Nicolaie) and Charles Gabet. First produced: Paris, 1877; London, 1878. English version by H. B. Farnie and Robert Reece. Set in 18th-century Normandy.*

In the village of Corneville there is a Legend of the Bells. The story goes that when the heir of the exiled Marquis de Corneville comes to reclaim his castle and estates, the ghostly bells of his neglected castle will welcome him. Gaspard, the castle's miserly caretaker, has made good use of supernatural superstitions in keeping strangers away from the place, where he lives with the Marquis's hoarded wealth, which he has appropriated as his own. His only companion is his niece Germaine, who is interested in Grenicheux, a young fisherman, supposed to have rescued her from drowning. Grenicheux knows he did not rescue her, but found her on the beach unconscious after she had been saved by another man, but is happy to take the credit.

The real rescuer had been the Corneville heir, making a secret visit to his estate. Now he returns to Corneville openly and sets up residence in the castle, despite Gaspard's attempts to dissuade him with warnings of ghosts and other dangers. Another local nobleman, the Comte de Lucenay, had also been banished years before, leaving behind a daughter, of whom no trace can now be found. The young Marquis finds birth documents which seem to point to his servant-girl from the village, Serpolette, as being Comte de Lucenay's missing daughter, and she is soon convincing herself that this is the truth.

The Marquis is not so sure. Meanwhile, determined to get at the truth of the reputed hauntings, he hides with friends and sees Gaspard drape a sheet about him and cavort at the window, and then trundle a suit of armour to and fro on a trolley, to give any watcher the impression of ghosts on the move. The Marquis decides to pay the old man out. He causes the bells to ring, and he and his party confront Gaspard in suits of ancient armour, posing as long-dead Cornevilles.

Gaspard is driven almost mad and reveals in his ramblings that the Comte's missing daughter is his purported niece, Germaine. The Marquis, who has by now recognised Germaine as the girl he had rescued from the sea and has dreamed of ever since, causes the Corneville bells to ring once more – as their wedding chimes.

PRINCIPAL NUMBERS

Act 1   'On billow rocking' (Grenicheux)
       'Legend of the bells' (Germaine and Chorus)
       'With joy my heart' (Marquis)
Act 2   'Let our torches' (Ensemble)
       'Silent Heroes' (Marquis)
Act 3   'The cider song' (Serpolette)

Rip van Winkle *by Robert Planquette, libretto by H. Meilhac, Philippe Gille and H. B. Farnie. First produced: London, 1882. Set in 18th-century America.*

Rip van Winkle (the character created by Washington Irving in 1819) is a seeming idler who does little else but roam the Catskill Mountains and poach the Hudson River, on which his home settlement of Sleepy Hollow lies near New York. Actually, he has been seeking a hoard of gold, buried by pirates. He finds it and pays off the lawyer Derrick van Slous who holds the mortgage on Rip's land and had been on the point of parting with it to the Government for a handsome sum. Thwarted of his profit, Derrick seizes on the fact that the coins in which Rip has paid him are French and reports Rip for being in the pay of Britain's enemy. Soldiers under a Captain Rowley are sent to arrest Rip, but aided by his wife, Gretchen, he slips away to hide in the Catskills.

The Catskills are an eerie region and villagers who accompany Gretchen to look for Rip there soon depart for home, leaving her to search alone. She finds him, but so does Derrick van Slous. Gretchen can only draw him away by pretending to be in love with him. Left alone, Rip undergoes a number of supernatural experiences which culminate in his drinking a great deal of schnapps and wine and, under the added influence of a spell cast by the shades of Hendrik Hudson and his crew, falling into a deep sleep.

It is twenty years before Rip van Winkle awakes. Now an old man, he returns to the settlement of Sleepy Hollow, which has become Wideawakeville. No one recognises Rip, despite his protestations. He learns that Gretchen is dead; their daughter Alice is now a young woman engaged to Hans van Slous, a naval lieutenant, son of Derrick, who is a rich political candidate. Mocked as a madman, Rip gradually manages to convince the villagers who he is, clinching his proof with a little song he had often sung to Alice and Hans when they were infants. The rascally Derrick van Slous, whose riches had been gained through Rip's absence, has to make over his property to the man he had wronged, and old Rip van Winkle gives the young lovers wealth as well as blessing.

PRINCIPAL NUMBERS

Act 1 'Oh, where's my girl?' (Rip)
       'Where flows the wild Mohawk' (Rip and Gretchen)
       Legend of the Catskills (Gretchen and Chorus)
       'The village well' (Katrina and Chorus)
Act 2 Lantern Chorus (Katrina and Gretchen)
       Echo Song (Rip and Chorus)
       Ninepins Song (2nd Lieut and Chorus)
Act 3 'Whatsoever may be won' (Katrina)
       'True love from o'er the sea' (Alice)
       'Truth in the well' (Rip)

Das Dreimäderlhaus *(Lilac Time), adapted from Franz Schubert's music by Heinrich Berté, libretto and lyrics by A. M. Willner and Heinz Reichert from a novel by R. H. Bartsch. First produced: Vienna, 1916; London, 1922. New English version by Philip Park (1971). Set in Vienna in 1826. (J.W.)*

The young composer Franz Schubert, at the height of his powers, is entertaining in the courtyard of his home, and the all-male company is enjoying wine and Baron Franz

89

Schober's account of his relationship with the opera singer Lucia Grisi. Three young sisters – Heiderl, Hederl and Hannerl Tschöll – enter, the two former with their boy friends, closely followed by their disapproving father. Schubert saves the young people from trouble by pretending to have invited Hannerl for a singing lesson. The old man is mollified, takes wine, and before long is giving the young lovers his blessing. Schubert meanwhile is all eyes for Hannerl, and when in due course he is asked to the Tschöll house to sing at the joint wedding celebration of Heiderl and Hederl, it is to Hannerl that his songs of love are addressed.

Lucia Grisi is amongst the guests, and jealously believing that Franz Schober is Hannerl's admirer, warns her to be wary of 'Franz', who will surely let her down. Hannerl supposes her to mean Franz Schubert. Surprised by her sudden coldness towards him, Schubert hands Schober his famous love song 'Impatience' ('Thine is my heart') and asks him to sing it to Hannerl for him. Unfortunately, the music and sentiments prove too potent. Hannerl believes them to be Schober's own declaration, and when he finds the two in each other's arms Schubert realises that he has made a tactical blunder.

Soon afterwards, Schober comes to ask Schubert a favour: he wants his friend to speak to Lucia Grisi on his behalf and break the news that he proposes to be faithful to his new love Hannerl. Lucia and Hannerl join them, the former full of recriminations, at which point it emerges that Schober's wooing had been on Schubert's behalf. Nevertheless, Hannerl is firmly in love with Schober now, and Franz Schubert can only console himself with the thought of the music that awaits the expression of his genius.

Act 1 'Just a little ring' (Heiderl, Hederl and Hannerl)
'Hark, hark, the lark!' (Ensemble)
'Under the lilac bough' (Ensemble)
'The golden song' (Hannerl and Schubert)
Act 2 'I am singing, I, your lover' (Schubert)
'Dream enthralling' (Schubert)
'The flower' (Hannerl and Schubert)
'Impatience' (Schubert)
Act 3 'My sweetest song of all' (Schubert)
'When the lilac bloom uncloses' (Hannerl and Schubert)

Ein Walzertraum *(A Waltz Dream) by Oscar Straus, libretto by Leopold Jacobson and Felix Dörmann. First produced: Vienna, 1907; London, 1908. English version by Basil Hood. Revised version first produced: Vienna, 1957. Set in a European state in contemporary period.*

At the castle of the Prince of Flausenthurm it is the wedding day of his daughter, the Princess Hélène, and Lieutenant Niki, a Viennese officer. Theirs is a love match, disappointing to the Prince and thoroughly distasteful to his cousin Count Lothar, who had hoped to gain Hélène himself. The hostile atmosphere has served to inhibit the lovers' feelings, and neither is able to demonstrate total affection for the other; both must hide behind semi-hostility, despite the persuasive efforts of Hélène's lady-in-waiting, Friederike von Insterburg. Although he has just been to the altar and it will soon be his wedding night, Niki insists to his aide and friend Lieutenant Montschi that they spend the evening in the public gardens near by, where they can hear the music of their beloved Vienna played by an all-girl band. Lothar overhears their plan and hurries to inform the Prince.

The haunting 'Waltz of my Dreams' proves to be prominent in the band's repertoire, and Niki is quickly attracted by its beautiful conductor, Franzi Steingruber. Lothar and the Prince, sidling in to try to catch Niki in some indiscretion, also succumb to the charms of members of the orchestra. Princess Hélène, who comes, unrecognised, looking for Niki for other reasons, asks Franzi if she has seen a young officer, and Franzi at once draws him to the spot by making her band repeat 'Waltz of my Dreams'; only to see him take Hélène into the waltz. When she tries to intervene she learns that they are the newly-married Princess and her Consort, and can only go back to her conducting as Niki and Hélène return to the castle.

Nevertheless, the couple's relationship is still not healed, until Hélène has the idea of asking Franzi to visit the castle daily and teach her the song to which Niki is evidently so susceptible. Franzi takes occasion to add some advice about the way to stimulate love. Hélène takes it, and, together with a successful rendering of 'Waltz of my Dreams', soon brings Niki home to her arms.

PRINCIPAL NUMBERS

Act 1   'The gay Hussar' (Friederike and others)
        'I don't care' (Niki)
        'A love of my own' (Hélène and Friederike)
        'Our unlucky dynasty' (Friederike, Niki and Prince)
        'Waltz of my dreams' (Niki and Montschi)
Act 2   'That's the life for me' (Franzi and Chorus)
        'My dear little maiden' (Franzi and Niki)
        'Piccolo, piccolo' (Franzi and Lothar)
Act 3   'Baroness and vagabond' (Franzi and Friederike)

Der Tapfere Soldat *(The Chocolate Soldier) by Oscar Straus, libretto by Rudolf Bernauer and Leopold Jacobson, based on George Bernard Shaw's play* Arms and the Man. *First produced: Vienna, 1908; London, 1910. English version by Stanislaus Stange. Set in Bulgaria in 1885.*

Colonel Popoff, of the Bulgarian army, is away at the Serbo-Bulgarian war, while his womenfolk – his wife Aurelia, daughter Nadina, and niece Mascha – wait at home. Nadina is yearning for her fiancé, Major Alexius Spiridoff, one of the chief heroes of the campaign, to return – 'Come, come! I love you only . . .' Instead, there arrives young Lieutenant Bumerli, an enemy officer on the run, who enters by Nadina's bedroom window and charms her into sheltering him. He tells her he is a Swiss, and, as if to prove it, consumes quantities of chocolate, so that she amusedly dubs him 'The Chocolate Soldier'. More disturbingly, he tells her that the celebrated cavalry charge on which her fiancé's fame rests had been entirely unintentional: his horse had run away with him, his men had followed, and their opponents had been unable to resist them because they had the wrong ammunition for their guns.

A patrol enters the house, searching for the fugitive. Nadina hides him until they have gone, then introduces him to her mother and cousin, who are equally charmed. They lend him a coat of Colonel Popoff's, into whose pocket each slips an inscribed photograph of herself. Then they give the exhausted man a comfortable bed and sing him to sleep with a lullaby.

Six months later the Bulgarian soldiers return from the war. Alexius begins to boast about his great deed, but Nadina makes it plain that she knows the truth. As he is wondering how she knows, Bumerli arrives to return the borrowed coat, just in time for Colonel Popoff's wife to produce this favourite garment for him. The three women remember the photographs in the pocket. It takes some elaborate business to retrieve them, and then jealousy is aroused as Nadina finds Mascha's and Mascha gets Nadina's, each with its affectionate inscription. Mascha, who is in love with Alexius, uses Nadina's photograph to convince Alexius of his fiancée's unfaithfulness. He accuses her, and is told that she is only too glad to be rid of him. Alexius proposes to fight Bumerli, but the duel does not materialise. Instead, Bumerli – who reveals that he is one of the wealthiest men in Switzerland – gets Nadina, and Alexius is content to settle for Mascha.

PRINCIPAL NUMBERS

Act 1 'My Hero – Come, come, I love you only' (Nadina)
'Sympathy' (Nadina and Bumerli)
'Seek the spy' (Ensemble)
Act 2 'Our heroes come – The Fatherland is free' (Chorus)
'Alexius the Brave' (Nadina and Alexius)
'Never was there such a lover' (Alexius and Nadina)
'The Chocolate Soldier' (Nadina and Ensemble)
'The tale of a coat' (Ensemble)
'That would be lovely' (Nadina and Bumerli)
Act 3 'Falling in love' (Alexius and Mascha)
The Letter Song (Bumerli)
The Letter Duet (Nadina and Bumerli)

Die Fledermaus *(The Bat) by Johann Strauss, libretto by Carl Haffner and Richard Genée after the comedy* Le Réveillon *by Meilhac and Halévy. First produced: Vienna, 1874; London, 1876. Modern English versions by Christopher Hassall and Edmund Tracey (1966, Sadler's Wells); Philip Park (1958) and George Melly (1970, Welsh National Opera). Set in contemporary Europe. (J.W.)*

Alfred, a professional singer, is laying siege to Rosalinda, the attractive wife of a wealthy man-about-town, Gabriel von Eisenstein. His big chance seems to have arrived when Eisenstein is sentenced to spend eight days in prison for insulting a policeman. Somewhat oddly, Eisenstein sets off for prison in full evening dress; but Rosalinda thinks no more of it when Alfred arrives and makes himself at home in her husband's dressing-gown. They settle down to a champagne supper and a cooing duet, but are interrupted by the arrival of Herr Frank, the prison governor, who has come to collect Eisenstein. Rosalinda's reputation seems about to be ruined. Her instinctive reaction is to insist that the man drinking champagne with her is her husband. Alfred is as amused as he is annoyed and allows himself to be taken away.

The reason, unknown to Rosalinda, for her real husband's departure in evening dress is that he has no intention of reporting to the prison until he has enjoyed a ball at Prince Orlofsky's, to which he has been invited by his old friend Dr Falke, with the promise that the girls from the ballet will be there. Also there, in one of her mistress's dresses, is Adele, Rosalinda's maid, whose sister is one of the dancers. Not recognising her, Eisenstein is soon making up to her.

The prison governor is a late arrival at the ball, pretending to be a French nobleman, and he and Eisenstein, who is posing as the Marquis Renard, become bosom friends over the champagne, without discovering each other's identities. The last guest to arrive is a bewitching Hungarian countess, who insists on keeping her features masked. Eisenstein makes for her at once, but she flirts with him at arm's length and teases him by snatching his watch and refusing to give it back.

The dancers entertain the company and, under the influence of the wine, Eisenstein amuses everyone with a story of a practical joke he had once played on his friend Falke which had much embarrassed the latter and left him with the nickname 'The Bat'. He little knows that this evening Falke is taking his revenge; for the 'Hungarian countess' is Rosalinda, brought by Falke for the purpose of showing her how unfaithful her husband can be. The festivities end with all the guests vowing eternal brotherhood and sisterhood, and, when six o'clock in the morning strikes, Eisenstein hastens away to prison without knowing how he has been duped.

Frosch, the gaoler, is very drunk and the arrival of an Eisenstein in addition to the one he already has locked up is beyond his comprehension. The governor is also too drunk to help much when he returns, and things become more complicated when various ladies start arriving looking for a non-existent Chevalier and a Marquis. Misleading tactics are no use – Falke and Rosalinda have concrete evidence in the form of Eisenstein's watch. When he finds that the countess for whom he is so ardent is his wife, he has to admit that she is worth it, and the work ends in yet another chorus in praise of the romantic properties of champagne.

PRINCIPAL NUMBERS

Act 1   'Love, no longer fly from me' (Alfred)
        'It's the talk of the town' (Falke and Eisenstein)

'And I must live eight long days' (Rosalinda, Adele
    and Eisenstein)
'A cage you keep for erring sheep' (Rosalinda,
    Alfred and Frank)
Act 2 'I always feel beholden (Chacun à son gout)'
    (Orlofsky)
'My dear Marquis' (Laughing Song) (Adele and
    Ensemble)
'What a tonic! What a beauty!' (Rosalinda and
    Einsenstein)
'Music of childhood, I hear you, forsaken (Czardas)'
    (Rosalinda)
'The glint of champagne glasses' (Ensemble)
Act 3 'Picture a coy village maiden' (Adele)

Cagliostro in Wien *(Cagliostro in Vienna) by Johann
Strauss, libretto by 'F. Zell' and Richard Genée; new version by
Gustave Quedenfeldt. First produced: Vienna, 1875; new
version, Danzig, 1941. (J.W.)*

Count Alessandro di Cagliostro, the Sicilian-born charlatan,
is visiting Vienna, ostensibly to practise his magic arts for
money. Assisted by his attractive mistress Lorenza, he is
drawing crowds and filling his pockets, despite the hostility
of the Commissioner of Public Morals, Baron Schnucki,
whom Lorenza easily manages to compromise.

But Cagliostro has a more serious purpose. It is to gain
audience with the Empress Maria Theresa and persuade her
to call off the intended betrothal of her son, the Archduke
Leopold, with the Infanta Marie Louise of Spain, in the
interests of France. He succeeds at last in convincing Baron
Schnucki of the genuineness of his powers and is granted an
interview with the Infanta herself, whom he hypnotises and

97

instructs to write a letter declining the betrothal. The letter falls into the hands of Baron Schnucki and a young officer, Lieutenant Feri von Lieven, who sets out to investigate Cagliostro's doings. Threatened with exposure by his own Lorenza, Cagliostro has to resort to bold measures. He informs the Empress that he can transmute base metals into gold. She agrees to visit his laboratory for a demonstration.

The gold Cagliostro produces consists of coins paid him by gullible women who have bought his rejuvenation mixture. His performance, however, is skilful enough to impress the Empress, and when Feri arrives to arrest the magician he is ordered to desist. But Cagliostro's troubles are not yet over. His male assistant, Blasoni, is also out to betray him by giving Feri documentary proof of his master's part in the political intrigue. This time the Empress orders Cagliostro's arrest. He gains his freedom in return for releasing the Infanta from his hypnotic spell, and makes his escape with Lorenza by balloon.

PRINCIPAL NUMBERS

'The Turks were here a hundred years' (Chorus)
Gypsy Song (Lorenza)
'Yes, Cagliostro is the man!' (Lorenza and Chorus)
'Who calls me?' (Ensemble)
'O my Misko, my trusty steed' (Feri)
'O sweet little word – Freedom!' (Ensemble)
'Could I but fly through life with you' (Frau Adami and Blasoni)
'Magician, listen to us!' (Cagliostro, Blasoni and Chorus)
'Love's happiness smiles on me' (Lorenza and Feri)
'Merrily drink the night away!' (Cagliostro and Ensemble)

Der Lustige Krieg *(The Merry War) by Johann Strauss, libretto by 'F. Zell' and Richard Genee. First produced: Vienna, 1881; London, 1882; new version by Wilhelm Sterk. Set in early 18th-century Tuscany. (J.W.)*

An unconventional war is being waged between the forces of Massa-Carrara and Genoa. The Massa-Carraran army is losing, perhaps because its commander-in-chief, the Countess Violetta Lomellini, and all its officers are women. Despite the loss of some hearts to their lady opponents, the Genoese have encircled them in their headquarters, and the Massa-Carrarans' only hope is the reinforcements promised by the Duke of Limburg. His price is marriage with the beautiful Violetta, who has never met him. Unfortunately, this plan is given away by a garrulous prisoner to Colonel Umberto Spinola, leader of the Genoese forces, who is easily able to capture the Duke's representative, Colonel von Scheelen, as he arrives to marry Violetta by proxy. Umberto encounters Violetta, falls in love with her at sight, and produces the captured Scheelen's papers, pretending to be him. Violetta is pleased to find her proxy husband handsome, and off they go to get married.

To add further verisimilitude to his deception, Umberto announces his master, the Duke of Limburg, at the wedding reception. Actually, the 'Duke' is another captive of the Genoese, Balthasar Groot, a Dutch tulip-grower travelling to Italy on business. Balthasar plays the part unwillingly, and even more so when his own wife, Else, arrives in search of him. She is plainly astonished, but has to support him by pretending not to know him, though the sight of the attractive Violetta at his side in the role of newly-wedded bride does not exactly delight her.

At length, Else can contain her jealousy no longer and tells Balthasar so in a conversation that is overheard. The story of Umberto's deception emerges in the course of it. Challenged as an enemy in the Massa-Carrarans' midst, he claims that he has married Violetta lawfully and is there as her husband. Before this paradox can be disputed, word comes that the two armies have made a truce, and peace and romance are free to reign.

PRINCIPAL NUMBERS

'No strife, no victory in this war' (Chorus)
'A flash, a crack, a little fear' (Umberto)
'It's lonely without one's husband' (Else)
'The cleverest one yields' (Marchese)
'Only for nature' (Marchese)
'The man I kissed' (Violetta and Umberto)
'Coming and going' (Ensemble)
'Haste to the altar' (Violetta and Umberto)
'The enemy I might have seen' (Ensemble)

Eine Nacht in Venedig *(A Night in Venice) by Johann Strauss, libretto by 'F. Zell' and Richard Genée. First produced: Berlin, 1883; London, 1944 (the new version made in 1923 by Hubert Marischka and Erich Wolfgang Korngold for the Vienna State Opera). English versions by Henrik Ege (1938); Sonny Miller and Eric Maschwitz (1953). Set in 18th-century Venice. (J.W.)*

The Duke of Urbino is notoriously interested in attractive women, single or married; and one husband who does not fancy taking his wife to the Duke's carnival night reception is old Senator Bartolomeo Delacqua, whose Barbara is many years his junior and outstandingly beautiful. He arranges to ship her off by gondola to her aunt's for the night, and take his cook, Ciboletta, to the party in her guise. The arrangement is overheard by Caramello, the Duke's barber. Knowing how much to his master's taste Barbara will be, he takes the place of the gondolier and ferries her to the ducal palace. Or, rather, he thinks he is doing so; for another deception is afoot. Barbara has an assignation with Enrico Piselli, a naval officer, and has arranged for a fisher-girl, Annina, to take her place in the gondola. So it is Annina whom Caramello conveys to the Duke's, while Barbara sneaks away to her meeting with Enrico, and the relieved Delacqua sets off to the reception with Ciboletta.

The Duke is much taken with Annina, and Caramello is much horrified when he sees her unmask – for she happens to be his own sweetheart. He dare not expose her, and she is not averse to making the most of the evening. Of course, when Delacqua arrives he introduces a second 'Barbara' to the scene. Annina whispers to the Duke that the old man has brought his cook in place of her, hoping to guard her from the Duke's attentions. The latter is much amused and plays up to the deception, treating Ciboletta courteously as Delacqua's wife, and managing to flirt with her and Annina at the same time. Jealous and frustrated, Caramello can only look on as a servant, together with Ciboletta's sweetheart Pappacoda, who has to help Caramello serve the supper. At least this enables them to keep the Duke in view until midnight, when he has to lead the carnival procession.

But all turns out well for the unhappy men. Ciboletta has managed to talk the Duke into making Pappacoda his chef. Caramello is given Annina back by his master, on condition that he marries her and becomes the Duke's factotum – a somewhat dubious gesture on the Duke's part, since it implies that the girl will always be close to him in the palace.

As for old Delacqua, distressed at the discovery that Barbara has never turned up at her aunt's at all, he is fobbed off with a tale of her having been kidnapped by a gondolier and rescued by Enrico.

PRINCIPAL NUMBERS

Act 1 ' 'Tis true, I am not very wise' (Ciboletta and Pappa-
        coda)
        'You do not fly to clasp me here' (Annina and Cara-
        mello)
Act 2 'True love is not my scheme' (Duke)
        'Listen, Annina, come in the gondola' (Annina and
        Caramello)
        'You promised when we meet again' (Duke and
        Annina)
Act 3 'All fair and beauteous to see' (Caramello)

Der Zigeunerbaron *(The Gypsy Baron) by Johann Strauss, libretto by Ignaz Schnitzer. First produced: Vienna, 1885; London, 1935. English versions by Henrik Ege (1934); Philip Park and Conrad Carter (1955); and Geoffrey Dunn (1964). Set in mid-19th-century Hungary. (J.W.)*

The handsome young Sandor Barinkay returns to his native Hungary from exile, to find his ancestral castle in ruins and its lands being used as a pig farm by a wealthy ignoramus, Zsupán, and as a gypsy encampment. Zsupán would be glad to see his daughter Arsena married to Sandor, but she is indifferent. The gypsies, whose friend his father had always been, swear allegiance to Sandor and acclaim him their Gypsy Baron. He is introduced to Saffi, the beautiful ward of Czipra, the gypsy queen. She sings a wild gypsy song and he falls in love with her. They marry under gypsy rites.

Czipra prophesies that Sandor will find a considerable treasure, hidden in the castle by his father at the time of their banishment. He does, and distributes it freely amongst his new friends. But a Royal Commissioner, Count Carnero, tries to call Sandor to account for consorting with a common gypsy girl. Czipra proves that Saffi is the natural daughter of the last pasha to rule in Hungary before the expulsion of the Turks, and so is of noble birth.

The governor of the province, Count Homonay, arrives with recruiting officers to raise troops for an imminent war with Spain. Any man who drinks a glass of recruiting wine thereby pledges himself to serve. The gypsies do so willingly, and the pig-breeder Zsupán unwittingly. Sandor is appointed to lead the gypsy contingent, but is denounced by Carnero. The governor, however, ignores him, and all march off to war.

Months later, in Vienna, crowds gather to see the victorious soldiers return. Zsupán is covered with medals which he has acquired rather than earned, but he confesses that Sandor had saved his life. The governor honours Sandor for courageous leadership, restores to him his father's wealth and confers on him the true title of Baron. Sandor insists that his style shall be 'Gypsy Baron', and anxiously looks round for Saffi. They are reunited and gaiety prevails.

PRINCIPAL NUMBERS

Act 1 Boatmen's Chorus (Ottokar, Czipra and Chorus)
'A suitor for a bride' (Ensemble)
'A moth who loves a flame' (Arsena)
'Do please taste it' (Maidens)
'There's no one in the world so fierce and faithful' (Saffi)

Act 2	'I dreamed I wandered by the river' (Saffi, Czipra and Barinkáy)
	'Who made us one' (Saffi, Barinkay and Chorus)
	'Come and join the gay Hussars' (Homonay and Chorus)
Act 3	'We're back again' (Zsupán, Ottokar and Chorus)
	'Sir, pray be kind' (Ensemble)
	'Marrying! Yes, yes!' (All)

Wiener Blut *(Vienna Blood) by Johann Strauss, adapted shortly after Strauss's death in 1899 by Adolf Müller Jr. Libretto by Viktor Léon and Leo Stein. First produced: Vienna, 1899. English version by Bruce Latham (1970). (J.W.)*

Balduin, Count Zedlau, Ambassador to Vienna of another European state, is thoroughly embroiled with women. He has a young wife, Gabriele, from whom he is living apart; a mistress, Franziska, a dancer, who is living with him at his villa outside Vienna; and a prospective mistress, Pepi Pleininger, a model, to whom he is at the stage of making overtures, but who, unknown to him, happens to be the fiancée of his valet, Josef. Prince Ypsheim-Gindelbach, Prime Minister of Balduin's state, arriving on an unexpected visit, is unaware of these ramifications, and takes the resident Franziska to be Balduin's wife, and Balduin's wife, who also happens to turn up, to be his mistress. Anxious not to antagonise his wife, Balduin begs the Prince to pretend that his (Balduin's) mistress is the Prince's own wife. The Prince is willing, but in his ignorance picks the wrong lady of the two, Gabriele, to introduce in the role.

But neither does Franziska know that Gabriele is the

Countess, imagining her to be merely a rival mistress. Each begs Balduin to take her out to supper at the casino at Hietzing, whereas he already has a rendezvous there that evening with Pepi. Prince Ypsheim produces further, almost inextricable, complications by embroiling Herr Kagler, Franziska's father, in the misunderstanding as to who is who and what is what. Gabriele encounters Pepi and takes her for Franziska, whom Pepi believes Gabriele to be. All this takes place at a ball in Vienna, so that the build-up to a situation of potential cataclysm is offset by the gaiety of the setting and the escapist rhythm of the waltz.

Balduin manages to get to Hietzing and meet Pepi. They retire into an arbour, only to be interrupted at once by Josef, the valet, come to warn his master that the other ladies are in pursuit. The discovery of his own fiancée alone with his master inevitably drags Josef into the all-round tangle, from which Balduin would be by now only too glad to extricate himself and settle down as a married man. His wife and his mistress have agreed upon the same notion for him. Franziska is happy to settle for old Prince Ypsheim instead. Josef accepts Balduin's assurance that he had not even reached the stage of kissing Pepi. Gabriele returns to her husband with joy.

PRINCIPAL NUMBERS

Act 1 'I seek him here, I seek him there' (Josef)
'Greeting, my dear child' (Count and Franziska)
'My sweet little dove' (Count and Josef)
Act 2 'Vienna blood' (Count and Countess)
'If I were your husband' (Count)
'My dear little treasure' (Count, Pepi and Josef)
Act 3 'Drink up! Drink up' (Sextet)

Die Schöne Galatea *(The Beautiful Galatea, or Ganymede and Galatea) by Franz von Suppé, libretto by Poly Henrion and Kohl von Kohlenegg. First produced: Berlin, 1865; London, 1872. Subsequently adapted freely by Theo Mackeben and Aldo von Pinelli into the version here summarised. Set in modern and ancient Greece. (J.W.)*

Present-day archaeologists have unearthed the statue of Galatea, which they allow to be viewed by a passing young married couple and their chauffeur, who clearly takes a lascivious delight both in the statue and in his employer's wife. Professor Agyris, in charge of the excavations, begins to tell them the legend of Pygmalion and Galatea, and his story is seen in 'flashback' to ancient times.

Midas, an art dealer, is facing demands from a crowd to produce the celebrated statue of Galatea he had promised to exhibit. His difficulty is that he cannot get it from Pygmalion, its sculptor, so he bribes Pygmalion's servant, Ganymede (corresponding to the chauffeur in the opening), to help. Ganymede smuggles Midas into Pygmalion's studio and shows him the beautiful statue, before Pygmalion (the young husband of the opening) enters, ejects Midas and sacks Ganymede. By an invocation to Venus, Pygmalion brings his statue to life: she is the young wife of the opening sequence.

Enchanted by life and by Pygmalion, Galatea is soon in his arms. But when Ganymede returns to the studio in Pygmalion's absence to collect his belongings, she is equally attracted by him. Midas sneaks in too, and is sufficiently taken to make her a present of an expensive bracelet. Pygmalion catches them all together. She tells him she proposes to elope with Ganymede. Pygmalion invokes

Venus's aid again, and the beautiful girl, together with Midas's bracelet, is turned back to stone.

The scene of the modern excavations returns. The young husband is viewing his chauffeur with renewed suspicion; but he relents from giving him the sack on the strength of it, and the three prepare to drive on and leave Galatea to the archaeologists.

PRINCIPAL NUMBERS

'Aurora's rays' (Chorus)
'To win a charming woman' (Ganymede)
'I feel love' (Pygmalion and Galatea)
'It's good to be alive' (Pygmalion)
'Once I was so loved' (Galatea)
'See the jewels' (Midas, Galatea and Ganymede)
Drinking Song (Ensemble)
'Ah, lovely luck!' (Ganymede and Galatea)
'Hither with joyous song' (Ensemble)

Boccaccio *by Franz von Suppé, libretto by 'F. Zell' and Richard Genée. First produced: Vienna, 1879; London, 1882. New English version by John Barker (1968). New version first produced: Vienna, 1951. Set in Florence in 1331.*

The young poet and story writer Giovanni Boccaccio is already famous and notorious in Florence. Women adore his sprightly tales, in most of which menfolk, especially possessive husbands, seem to come off worst; so men are decidedly not amongst Boccaccio's admirers. One girl above the others is taken with the young man's handsome gaiety. She is Fiametta, adopted daughter of the grocer Lambertuccio and his wife Petronella, but actually the natural daughter of the Duke of Tuscany, who has fostered her out to the worthy couple.

Having failed to get a magistrates' order that Boccaccio must leave Florence, the citizens take the law into their own hands and beat him. Their mistaken victim, however, is a young man resembling Boccaccio, who is in fact Pietro, Prince of Palermo, who is in Florence to find Fiametta, the bride he has been promised. Luckily for his persecutors, he is in a pleasure-seeking mood, forgives them, and proceeds to make love to Isabella, wife of the cooper Lotteringhi. He is nearly caught when her husband returns unexpectedly, and only the ingenious use of an unfinished barrel – and Isabella's willing co-operation – saves him and enables the love-making to continue.

Boccaccio similarly gulls Lambertuccio by persuading him to climb up into a tree and see for himself that it has magical properties. All the grocer sees from his vantage point is his wife being made love to by a student, Leonetto, and his adopted daughter receiving similar treatment from Boccaccio.

The rage of the respective worthies when they find how they have been tricked results in another thrashing, this time erroneously administered to the Duke of Tuscany, who is in the district incognito to look for his daughter and take her away to be married. Fiametta is sought out at length, but only agrees to leave the district when Boccaccio assures her that wherever she goes, he will follow.

He does follow her to the Duke's palace, where he is to produce a comedy for the guests' entertainment. Prince Pietro, seeing that Fiametta and Boccaccio are truly in love, generously withdraws his claim to her, but the Duke seems adamant that the arranged marriage must take place.

Boccaccio's literary skill wins the day. His comedy allegorises the situation in a way that the Duke cannot fail to see. He gives his final judgement, that Boccaccio be sentenced to serve a life-term – as Fiametta's husband.

PRINCIPAL NUMBERS

Act 1 'Hither, girls and boys!' (Chorus)
'From thy placid slumbers' (Ensemble)
'Let me relate' (Boccaccio and Chorus)
'Young love' (Fiametta and Boccaccio)
Act 2 'My soul, my star,' (Boccaccio, Pietro and Leonetto)
Letter trio (Fiametta, Isabella and Petronella)
'I'm but country-bred' (Boccaccio)
Act 3 'Forget not to forget!' (Boccaccio)
'Oh mountains blue!' (Boccaccio and Leonetto)
'When first these eyes' (Fiametta and Boccaccio)

Der Vogelhändler *(The Bird-Seller) by Karl Zeller, libretto by Moritz West and Ludwig Held. First produced: Vienna, 1891; London, 1895. New version by Bruce Walker and Fred S. Tysh. Set in the Rhine valley, early 18th century. (J.W.)*

Baron Weps has been sent by his master, the Prince, to organise a boar hunt. There is only one snag: no boar are left in the district. The local burgomaster, Schneck, rather than lose the Prince's patronage, offers to organise some belligerent sows, and bribes Weps to sustain the deception. Weps is only too co-operative. He needs the money to help his spendthrift nephew Stanislaus, a handsome Guards officer, to pay his debts. When the Prince suddenly cancels the hunt, Weps, rather than pay back Schneck's bribe, keeps

109

the cancellation quiet and gets Stanislaus to turn up masquerading as the Prince.

Stanislaus does so and is visited soon after arrival by Christel, the young postmistress, to petition 'the Prince' to appoint Adam, her fiancé, as director of the Royal Zoo. Stanislaus accedes. But Adam, a bird-seller by trade, is not pleased. He suspects that Christel has granted the Prince certain improper favours as the price of the appointment – an unfounded jealousy made all the less worthy by his own flirtation with another girl, Marie. This, in fact, is the Princess Marie, who has come to the district incognito to keep an eye on her consort, whose fidelity she doubts. Not knowing of the cancellation of the hunt, she believes it is her Prince who has received Christel in his lodgings; she therefore willingly reciprocates Adam's attentions with a gift of roses and arranges for him to go to the palace for an interview for the job of zoo director.

He is appointed, despite his attempts to make a bad impression on the interviewing professors, Süffle and Würmchen. Still seeking proof of the Prince's infidelity, the Princess Marie persuades Christel to point out the man who had interviewed her in his lodgings and tried (in vain, as it happens) to kiss her. It is, of course, Stanislaus to whom she points. He has arrived at the palace with the ageing Countess Adelaide, whom his uncle has persuaded him to marry to raise money to settle his huge debts. Now that the truth is out, Adam is invited to pass judgement on the man who had wronged him. He orders Stanislaus to resign from his regiment or marry Christel, whom Adam declares he no longer wants. Stanislaus chooses the latter course.

Adam has by now seen that the peasant girl Marie and the Princess are the same person, and his affection for Christel returns, especially when he overhears her refusing to marry

Stanislaus. Adam and Christel are reunited, and Stanislaus is paid out by having to proceed with his marriage to his old countess.

PRINCIPAL NUMBERS

Act 1   'I hold the reins' (Christel and Ladies)
   'Build a nest' (Adam and Chorus)
   'When you're near' (Adam and Christel)
   'Roses mean Love' (Adam and Marie)
Act 2   'If Love should ever cross my way' (Prince, Marie and Chorus)
   'One day sunshine, one day rain' (Adam, Christel and Tyroleans)
   'Nightingale' (Adam and Ensemble)
Act 3   'Catch your man' (Stanislaus, Adelaide and Weps)
   'Life can be a fairy-tale' (Marie, Christel, Prince, Adam and Chorus)

Discography

For the details included in this discography I am largely indebted to Mr Frank Rogers, of The Gramophone Exchange Limited, 80–82 Wardour Street, London WIV 4BD (telephone 01-437 5313). All are relatively modern recordings, on long-playing discs, of complete versions (marked *comp*) or substantial vocal selections. Of course, a mass of recordings exists of individual songs, overtures and vocal and orchestral *potpourris,* but the inclusion of these would require far more space than is available.

A symbol after each entry indicates the language in which the recording is sung: (F)=French, (G)=German, (R)=Russian, (E)=English, (S)=Swedish. No record numbers or details of labels are shown, partly because the European numbering system is undergoing radical changes, but also because recordings originating in one country under a certain label and serial numbers are often reissued elsewhere, quite differently labelled and numbered. Mention of the principal artists is enough for any good record dealer to go upon; but in case of difficulty I would refer the reader to Frank Rogers, whose knowledge of the international market is profound.

AUBERGE DU CHEVAL BLANC, L' (See IM WEISSEN RÖSSL)
BARON TZIGANE, LE (See ZIGEUNERBARON, DER)

BAT, THE (See FLEDERMAUS, DIE)

BEAUTIFUL GALATEA (See SCHÖNE GALATEA, DIE)

BEGGAR STUDENT, THE (See BETTELSTUDENT, DER)

BELLE HÉLÈNE, LA, Offenbach: Devos, Doniat, Berton.
Cond. Gressier (F)
Blackham, Miller, Nash, Kern. Cond. Matheson (E)

BELLS OF CORNEVILLE, THE (See CLOCHES DE
CORNEVILLE, LES)

BETTELSTUDENT, DER, Millöcker: (comp.) Anday, Lipp,
Rethy, Christ, Wächter, Preger. Cond. Paulik (G)
(comp.) Gueden, Schock, Ollendorf. Cond. Stolz (G)
Litz, Streich, Holm, Gedda, Unger, Prey. Cond. Allers (G)
Tauber, Schwartz, Schutzendorf. Cond. Romner (G)
(coupled with Casanova – Strauss)
Konya, Schneider. Cond. Marszalek (G)
Konetzni, Gueden, Schädle, Schock, Minich, Ollen-
dorf. Cond. Stolz (G)
Draksler, Rysanek, Terkal. Cond. Richter (G) (coupled
with Im Weissen Rössl (q.v.))
Talmer, Konya, Fehringer. Cond. Marszalek (G) (coupled
with Schwarzwaldmädel – Jessel)
Oelke, Schirrmacher, Vantin. Cond. Melichar (G)
Köth, Schock, Topper, Wunderlich. Cond. Schmidt-
Boelcke (G)
Anday, Lipp, Rethy. Cond. Pavlic (G)
Schoner, Camer, Grobe. Cond.? (G) (coupled with
Vogelhändler, Der (q.v.))

BIRD-SELLER, THE (See VOGELHÄNDLER, DER)

BOCCACCIO, Suppé: Roon, Kmentt, Preger. Cond. Paulik (G)
Schock, Holm, Schirrmacher. Cond. Fox (G)
Rothenberger, Hoppe, Prey. Cond. Michalsky (G)
(coupled with Gasparone – Millöcker)
Berry, Roon, Kmentt, Scheyer. Cond. Paulik (G)

CAGLIOSTRO IN WIEN: Strauss: Wächter, Ludwig, Kmentt. *Cond.* Salmhofer (G) (coupled with *Lustige Krieg, Der* (q.v.))
CASTLES IN THE AIR (See FRAU LUNA)
CHAUVE-SOURIS, LA (See FLEDERMAUS, DIE)
CHOCOLATE SOLDIER, THE (See TAPFERE SOLDAT, DER)
CHANSON D'AMOUR (See DREIMÄDERLHAUS, DAS)
CIRCUS PRINCESS, THE (See ZIRKUSPRINZESSIN, DIE)
CLOCHES DE CORNEVILLE, LES, Planquette: *(comp.)*
    Petrov, Vermel, Sokolovskaya. *Cond.* Pyatigorsky (R)
    Dens, Peyron. *Cond.* Gressier (F)
    Dens, Micheau, Sénéchal. *Cond.* Pourcel (F)
COMTE DE LUXEMBOURG, LE (See GRAF VON LUXEMBURG, DER)
COUNT OF LUXEMBOURG, THE (See GRAF VON LUXEMBURG, DER)
COUNTESS MARITZA (See GRÄFIN MARIZA, DIE)
COUSIN FROM NOWHERE, THE (See VETTER AUS DINGSDA, DER)
CZARDASFÜRSTIN, DIE, Kálmán: *(comp.)* Rothenberger, Gedda. *Cond.* Mattes (G)
    (comp.) Yakovenko, Nelepp, Kazanskaya. *Cond.* Samosud (R)
    Schock, Schramm, Gruber. *Cond.* Stolz (G)
    Barabas, Schock, Glawitsch. *Cond.* Fox (G) (coupled with *Gräfin Mariza, Die* (q.v.))
    Knittal, Hoppe, Camer. *Cond.?* (G) (coupled with *Frau Luna* (q.v.))
    Talmer, Holm, Hofmann. *Cond.* Marszalek (G) (coupled with *Zigeunerbaron, Der* (q.v.))
CZAREVITCH, THE (See ZAREWITSCH, DER)
DOLLARPRINZESSIN, DIE, Fall: Bartel, Bartos, Hofmann. *Cond.* Marszalek (G) (coupled with *Zirkusprinzessin, Die* (q.v.))

Barabas, Hoppe, Görner. *Cond.* Michalsky (G)

DREIMÄDERLHAUS, DAS, Schubert: *(comp.)* Doniat, Dachary, Mallabrera. *Cond.* Etcheverry (F). Titled *Chanson d'Amour.*

Söner, Grobe. *Cond.* Hagestedt (G) (coupled with *Friederike* (q.v.))

Roon, Meyer-Welfing, Oeggl. *Cond.* Pauspertl (G)

Grobe, Schoner, Camer. *Cond.?* (G) (coupled with *Im Weissen Rössl* (q.v.))

Köth, Schock, Kunz. *Cond.* Fox (G)

DRUM-MAJOR'S DAUGHTER, THE (See FILLE DU TAMBOUR-MAJOR, LA)

DUBARRY, DIE, Millöcker: Sprierenburg, Tertal. *Cond.* Richter (G) (coupled with *Schön ist die Welt* (q.v.))

Köth, Wilhelm. *Cond.* Fox (G) (coupled with *Rose von Stambul, Die* – Fall*)*

FAIR HELEN, THE (See BELLE HÉLÈNE, LA)

FILLE DE MADAME ANGOT, LA, Lecocq: Dens, Peyron, Dachary. *Cond.* Gressier (F)

Tsenin, Shumskaya, Nelepp. *Cond.* Akulov (R)

FILLE DU TAMBOUR-MAJOR, LA, Offenbach: Chatel, Sautereau, Dens. *Cond.* Nuvolone (F)

FLEDERMAUS, DIE, Strauss: *(comp.)* Rothenberger, Wächter, Konya, Leigh. *Cond.* Danon (G)

(comp.) Gueden, Patzak, Dermota, Lipp. *Cond.* Krauss (G)

(comp.) Kmentt, Gueden, Zampieri, Köth. *Cond.* Karajan (G)

(comp.) Schock, Lipp, Berry, Holm, *Cond.* Stolz (G)

(comp.) Schwarzkopf, Gedda. *Cond.* Karajan (G)

Holm, Lipp, Schock. *Cond.* Stolz (G)

Konya, Hofmann, Schneider. *Cond.* Marszalek (G) (coupled with *Wiener Blut* (q.v.))

Nash, Young, Elliott, Studholme. *Cond.* Tausky (E)

Brumaire, Berton, Forli. *Cond.* Pourcel (F)

FRASQUITA, Lehár: Murano, Dassary, Broissin. *Cond.* Cariven (F)

FRAU LUNA, Lincke: Köth, Hoppe, Litz. *Cond.* Mattes (G) (coupled with *Lysistrata* – Lincke, and *Im Reiche des Indra* – Lincke)

Knittel, Hoppe, Schollwer. *Cond.?* (G) (coupled with *Czardasfürstin, Die* (q.v.))

Schirrmacher, Schollwer, Lins. *Cond.* Schroder (G)

Talmer, Holm, Fehringer. *Cond.* Marszalek (G) (coupled with *Hochzeitnacht im Paradies* – Schroder)

FRIEDERIKE, Lehár: Schock, Schramm. *Cond.* Schmidt-Boelke (G) (coupled with *Schön ist die Welt* (q.v.))

Söner, Grober, Friedauer. *Cond.* Hagestedt (G) (coupled with *Dreimäderlhaus, Das* (q.v.))

Barabas. *Cond.* ? (G) (coupled with *Schwarzwaldmädel* – Jessel)

Knittel, Camer, Hoppe. *Cond.?* (G)

GIUDITTA, Lehár: *(comp.)* Gueden, Loose, Kmentt, Berry. *Cond.* Moralt (G)

Geszty, Schock. *Cond.* Schmidt-Boelcke (G)

Rothenberger, Gedda, Görner. *Cond.* Mattes (G) (coupled with *Wiener Blut* (q.v.))

GLADA ÄNKAN (See LUSTIGE WITWE, DIE)

GRAF VON LUXEMBURG, DER, Lehár: *(comp.)* Gedda, Popp, Holm. *Cond.* Mattes (G)

Schock, Schramm, Krukowski. *Cond.* Stolz (G)

Köth, Hildebrand, Schock. *Cond.* Fox (G)

Talmer, Fehringer, Camer. *Cond.* Marszalek (G) (coupled with *Lustige Witwe, Die,* (q.v.))

Berton, Dens, Roux. *Cond.* Nuvolone (F). Under the title *Le Comte de Luxembourg.*

Söderström, Grundén. *Cond.* Kjerrmans (s). Under the

title *Greven av Luxemburg* (coupled with *Lustige Witwe, Die* (q.v.))

GRÄFIN MARIZA, DIE, Kálmán: *(comp.)* Richter, Torok, Ritzmann. *Cond.* Kegel (G)

(comp.) Yakovenko, Matveyev, Shevtsova. *Cond.* Silantyev (R)

Schramm, Gruber, Schock. *Cond.* Stolz (G)

Schock, Barabas, Glawitsch. *Cond.* Fox (G) (coupled with *Czardasfürstin, Die* (q.v.))

Grobe, Shirrmacher, Schoner. *Cond.* Schmidt-Boelcke (G)

Talmer, Bartos, Bartel. *Cond.* Marszalek (G) (coupled with *Viktoria und ihr Husar* (q.v.))

GRANDE-DUCHESSE DE GÉROLSTEIN, LA, Offenbach: Lublin, Amade, Benoit. *Cond.* Marty (F)

Zareska, Prévet, Dran, Riley, Théry. *Cond.* Leibowitz (F)

GREVEN AV LUXEMBURG (See GRAF VON LUXEMBURG, DER)

GYPSY BARON, THE (See ZIGEUNERBARON, DER)

GYPSY LOVE (See ZIGEUNERLIEBE)

GYPSY PRINCESS, THE (See CZARDASFÜRSTIN, DIE)

HELEN OR TAKEN FROM THE GREEK (See BELLE HÉLÈNE, LA)

IM WEISSEN RÖSSL, Benatzky: *(comp.)* Hallstein, Köth, Alexander, Schock. *Cond.* Fehring (G)

(comp.) Bourvil, Forli, Dens, Germain. *Cond.* Nuvolone (F). Under the title *L'Auberge du Cheval Blanc*.

Knittel, Kuchar, Kolmann. *Cond.* Fessel (G)

Haas, Ott, Klug, Minich. *Cond.* Bibl (G)

Briner, Christ, Minich. *Cond.* Michalsky (G)

Staal, Rothenberger, Friedauer. *Cond.* Schmidt-Boelcke (G)

Hubner, Moogk, Dotzer. *Cond.* Knapp (G) (coupled with *Maske in Blau* – Raymond)

Liebesberg, Spierenburg, Braun. *Cond.* Richter (G)

(coupled with *Bettelstudent, Der* (q.v.))

Hoppe, Hellwig, Rothenberger. *Cond. ?* (G) (coupled with *Dreimäderlhaus, Das* (q.v.))

Talmer, Schorg, Groh. *Cond.* Marszalek (G) (coupled with *Saison in Salzburg* – Raymond)

Pelters, Elkin, Stack. *Cond. ?* (G)

JUDITH (See GIUDITTA)

LANDDESLÄCHELNS, DAS, Lehár: *(comp.)* Gedda, Rothenberger, Holm. *Cond.* Mattes (G)

(comp.) Schwarzkopf, Gedda, Kunz. *Cond.* Ackermann (G)

(comp.) Rothenberger, Anders, Dietrich. *Cond.* Feltz (G)

Di Stefano, Koller, Goodall. *Cond.* Lambrecht (G)

Poncet, Doria, Gui. *Cond.* Etcheverry. (F). Under the title *Le Pays du Sourire.*

Vanzo, Duval. *Cond.* Chevreux (F). Under the title *Le Pays du Sourire.*

Muszely, Wunderlich, Friedauer. *Cond.* Michalsky (G) (coupled with *Zarewitsch, Der* (q.v.))

Schramm, Schock, Gruber. *Cond.* Stolz (G)

Hubner, Moogk, Kraft. *Cond.?* (G) (coupled with *Die Blume von Hawaii* – Abraham)

Köth, Schock, Hildebrand. *Cond.* Schüchter (G) (coupled with *Zarewitsch, Der* (q.v.))

Talmer, Holm, Konya, Alexander. *Cond.?* (G) (coupled with *Zarewitsch, Der* (q.v.))

Dens, Devos, Noguera, Berton. *Cond.* Cariven (F). Under the title *Le Pays du Sourire.*

Craig, Fretwell, Bronhill. *Cond.* Tausky (E). Under the title *Land of Smiles.*

LUSTIGE KRIEG, DER, Strauss: Kmentt, Ludwig, Wächter. *Cond.* Strauss (G) (coupled with *Cagliostro in Wien* (q.v.)) Rakov, Petrinenko. *Cond.* Tolba (R)

LUSTIGE WITWE, DIE, Lehár: *(comp.)* Schwarzkopf, Gedda, Wächter. *Cond.* Matacic (G)

(comp.) Gueden, Kmentt, Loose, Grunden. *Cond.* Stolz (G)

(comp.) Schramm, Schock, Christ. *Cond.* Stolz (G)

(comp.) Dens, Lafaye, Mallabrera. *Cond.* Leenart (F). Under the title *La Veuve Joyeuse.*

Reardon, Della Casa, Hurley, Davis. *Cond.* Allers (E). Under the title *The Merry Widow.*

Gedda, Köth, Ilosfalvy. *Cond.* Mattes (G)

Schock, Schramm, Kusche. *Cond.* Stolz (G)

Talmer, Bartos, Fehringer. *Cond.* Marszalek (G) (coupled with *Graf von Luxemburg, Der* (q.v.))

Munsel, Porreta, Allers. *Cond.?* (E). Under the title *The Merry Widow.*

Dens, Vivalda, Amade. *Cond.* Pourcel (F). Under the title *La Veuve Joyeuse.*

Jansen, Duvaleix, Devos, Duval. *Cond.* Gressier (F). Under the title *La Veuve Joyeuse.*

Bronhill, Round, Price. *Cond.* Reid (E). Under the title *The Merry Widow.*

Bronhill, Brett, Hughes, Howard. *Cond.* Tausky (E). Under the title *The Merry Widow.*

Grudén, Sternquist, Gerthel, Kjerrman. *Cond.* Kjerrmans (s). Under the title *Glada Änkan* (coupled with *Graf von Luxemburg, Der* (q.v.))

MADAME ANGOT'S DAUGHTER (See FILLE DE MADAME ANGOT, LA)

MADAME POMPADOUR, Fall: Lohe, Ksirowa, Westhoff. *Cond.* Dobrindt (G)

MAM'ZELLE NITOUCHE, Hervé: Peyron, Roger, Devos. *Cond.* Cariven (F)

MASCOTTE, LA, Audran: Dens, Berton, Devons. *Cond.* Gressier (F)

MERRY WAR, THE (See LUSTIGE KRIEG, DER)

MERRY WIDOW, THE (See LUSTIGE WITWE, DIE)

MONSIEUR BEAUCAIRE, Messager: Dens, Lenoty, Berton. *Cond.* Gressier (F)

NACHT IN VENEDIG, EINE, Strauss: *(comp.)* Streich, Rothenberger, Gedda. *Cond.* Allers (G)

   Schock, Wunderlich, Otto. *Cond.* ? (G)

   Curzi, Schock, Köth, Schirrmacher. *Cond.* Schmidt-Boelcke (G)

   Hallstein, Bartos, Konya. *Cond.* Marszalek (G) (coupled with *Paganini* (q.v.))

   Rethy, Friedrich, Preger. *Cond.* Paulik (G)

   Gedda, Kunz, Schwarzkopf. *Cond.* Ackermann (G) (coupled with *Wiener Blut* (q.v.))

   Schoner, Hoppe. *Cond.* ? (G) (coupled with *Wiener Blut* (q.v.))

   Streich, Litz, Gedda, Curzi. *Cond.* Allers (G)

   Hayward, Smith, Martin. *Cond.?* (E). Under the title *A Night in Venice.*

NIGHT IN VENICE, A (See NACHT IN VENEDIG, EINE)

ORPHÉE AUX ENFERS, Offenbach: Doniat, Roux, Berton. *Cond.* Gressier (F)

   Terkal, Leibesberg. *Cond.* Richter (G). Under the title *Orpheus in der Unterwelt.*

   Apelt, Schreier, Vulpius. *Cond.* Hanell (G). Under the title *Orpheus in der Underwelt.*

   Bronhill and other artists. *Cond.* Faris (E). Under the title *Orpheus in the Underworld.*

ORPHEUS IN DER UNTERWELT (See ORPHÉE AUX ENFERS)

ORPHEUS IN THE UNDERWORLD (See ORPHÉE AUX ENFERS)

PAGANINI, Lehár: Schramm, Christ, Schock. *Cond.* Stolz (G).
  Hoppe, Schoner. *Cond. ?* (G)
  Talmer, Holm, Konya. *Cond. ?* (G) (coupled with *Nacht in Venedig, Eine* (q.v.))
  Dens, Forli, Sautereau. *Cond.* Pourcel (F)

PARISER LEBEN (See VIE PARISIENNE, LA)

PAYS DU SOURIRE, LE (See LAND DES LÄCHELNS, DAS)

PÉRICHOLE, LA, Offenbach: Lafaye, Amade. *Cond.* Markevitch (F)

PETIT DUC, LE, Lecocq: Clement, Berton, Renaux. *Cond.* Gressier (F)

P'TITES MICHU, LES, Messager: Berton, Renaux, Maurane. *Cond.* Gressier (F)

RIP VAN WINKLE, Planquette: Dens, Berton, Benoit, Vivalda. *Cond.* Gressier (F)

SCHÖN IST DIE WELT, Lehár: Rysanek, Terkal, Spierenburg. *Cond.* Richter (G) (coupled with *Dubarry, Die* (q.v.))
  Schock, Geszty. *Cond.* Schmidt-Boelcke (G) (coupled with *Friederike* (q.v.))

SCHÖNE GALATEA, DIE, Suppé: Roon, Kmentt, Preger. *Cond.* Paulik (G)

TAPFERE SOLDAT, DER, Straus: Stevens, Merrill, Palmer. *Cond.* Engel (E). Under the title *The Chocolate Soldier.*

VÉRONIQUE, Messager: *(comp.)* Mesple, Dens, Guiot. *Cond.* Hartemann (F)

VETTER AUS DINGSDA, DER, Künneke: Holm, Schock, Schirrmacher. *Cond.* Schmidt-Boelcke (G)
  Köth, Schock, Strienz. *Cond.* Schmidt-Boelcke (G)
  Köth, Hoppe, Bohme. *Cond.* Mattes (G) (coupled with

Das Schwarzwaldmädel – Jessel)

Talmer, Fehringer, Holm. *Cond. ?* (G) (coupled with *Vogelhändler, Der* (q.v.))

VEUVE JOYEUSE, LA (See LUSTIGE WITWE, DIE)

VIE PARISIENNE, LA, Offenbach: *(comp.)* Della Casa, Hallstein, Schock, Wächter. *Cond.* Allers (G). Under the title *Pariser Lieben.*

Wächter, Della Casa, Alexander. *Cond.* Allers (G). Under the title *Pariser Leben.*

Roux, Clement, Dachary. *Cond.* Gressier (F)

Bronhill, Miller, Shilling. *Cond.* Faris (E)

VIENNA BLOOD (See WIENER BLUT)

VIKTORIA UND IHR HUSAR, Abraham: Niessner, Brauner, Equiluz. *Cond.* Gruber (G) (coupled with *Die Blume von Hawaii* – Abraham)

Gruber, Schramm, Schock. *Cond.* Schmidt-Boelcke (G) (coupled with *Die Blume von Hawaii* – Abraham)

Barabas, Knittel, Hoppe. *Cond.* Graunke (G) (coupled with *Die Blume von Hawaii* – Abraham)

Bartos, Schoner, Grober. *Cond. ?* (G) (coupled with *Die Blume von Hawaii* – Abraham)

Konya, Bartos, Hofmann. *Cond.* Marszalek (G) (coupled with *Gräfin Mariza, Die* (q.v.))

VOGELHÄNDLER, DER, Zeller: Minich, Kusche, Gueden, Terkal. *Cond.* Breuer (G)

Knittel, Hoppe, Görner. *Cond.* Michalsky (G) (coupled with *Der Fidele Bauer* – Fall)

Köth, Schock, Holm. *Cond.* Fox (G)

Hallstein, Talmer, Fehringer. *Cond.* Marszalek (G) (coupled with *Vetter aus Dingsda, Der* (q.v.))

Schoner, Camer, Grobe. *Cond. ?* (G) (coupled with *Bettelstudent, Der* (q.v.))

Barabas, Gruber, Schwaiger. *Cond.* Schmidt-Boelcke (G)

Stratas, Popp, Dallapozza. *Cond.* Bauer-Theussl (G)

Maslennikova, Timchenko, Vishnevskaya. *Cond.* Stolyarov (R)

WALTZ DREAM, A (See WALZERTRAUM, EIN)

WALZERTRAUM, EIN, Straus: *(comp.)* Gedda, Rothenberger, Anheisser. *Cond.* Mattes (G)

Talmer, Konya, Alexander. *Cond.* Marszalek (G) (coupled with *Gasparone* – Millöcker)

Bronhill, Hughes, Grimaldi. *Cond.* Collins (E)

WHITE HORSE INN (See IM WEISSEN RÖSSL)

WIENER BLUT, Strauss: *(comp.)* Lipp, Gueden, Schock. *Cond.* Stolz (G)

(comp.) Schwarzkopf, Gedda. *Cond.* Ackermann (G)

(comp.) Hoppe, Hauser, Richter. *Cond.* ? (G)

Gedda, Schwarzkopf, Kunz. *Cond.* Ackermann (G) (coupled with *Nacht in Venedig, Eine* (q.v.))

Gueden, Grobe, Schoner. *Cond.*? (G) (coupled with *Nacht in Venedig, Eine* (q.v.))

Talmer, Konya, Alexander. *Cond.* Marszalek (G) (coupled with *Fledermaus, Die* (q.v.))

Gedda, Rothenberger, Görner. *Cond.* Mattes (G) (coupled with *Giuditta* (q.v.))

ZAREWITSCH, DER, Lehár: *(comp.)* Gedda, Streich, Freidauer. *Cond.* Mattes (G)

Della Casa, Roswaenge, Jungwirth. *Cond.* Reinshagen (G)

Schock, Holm, Mercker. *Cond.* Stolz (G)

Wunderlich, Muszely. *Cond.* Michalsky (G) (coupled with *Land des Lächelns, Das* (q.v.))

Köth, Schock. *Cond.* Schüchter (G) (coupled with *Land des Lächelns, Das* (q.v.))

Schoner, Schirrmacher, Traxel. *Cond.* Schmidt-Boelcke (G)

Talmer, Bartos, Bartel. *Cond. ?* (G) (coupled with *Land des Lächelns, Das* (q.v.))

ZIGEUNERBARON, DER, Strauss: *(comp.)* Loose, Patzak, Zadek. *Cond.* Krauss (G)

(comp.) Bumbry, Streich, Gedda, Prey. *Cond.* Allers (G)

(comp.) Wächter, Schock, Schädle, Hazy. *Cond.* Stolz (G)

(comp.) Schwarzkopf, Gedda. *Cond.* Ackermann (G)

(comp.) Loose, Scheyer, Kmentt, Preger. *Cond.* Paulik (G)

Wächter, Schock, Hazy. *Cond.* Stolz (G)

Konya, Hofmann, Schneider. *Cond.* Marszalek (G) (coupled with *Czardasfürstin, Die* (q.v.))

Köth, Bartos, Schneider. *Cond. ?* (G) (coupled with *Gasparone* – Millöcker)

Preger, Braun, Christ. *Cond.* Moralt (G) (coupled with *Polenblut* – Nedbal)

Köth, Schock, Kusche, Strienz. *Cond.* Schmidt-Boelcke (G)

Micheau, Chauvet, Benoit. *Cond.* Lombard (F). Under the title *Le Baron Tzigane*.

Sadler's Wells Company. *Cond.* Tausky (E)

ZIGEUNERLIEBE, Lehár: *(comp.)* Groh, Seegers, Appelt. *Cond.* Dobrindt (G)

(comp.) Yakovenko, Potapovskaya, Ivanovsky. *Cond.* Kovalev (R)

Schock, Schramm, Katona. *Cond.* Stolz (G)

Hoppe, Barabas, Friedauer. *Cond.* Michalsky (G) (coupled with *Dollarprinzessin, Die* (q.v.))

ZIRKUSPRINZESSIN, DIE, Kálmán: Schock, Gruber, Schramm. *Cond.* Stolz (G)

Bartel, Bartos. *Cond.* Marszalek (G) (coupled with *Dollarprinzessen, Die* (q.v.))

Barabas, Koster, Wehofschitz. *Cond.* Fox (G)

Uzunov, Yakovenko. *Cond.* Silantyev (R)